TERRORISM

WHAT EVERYONE NEEDS TO KNOW®

TERRORISM

WHAT EVERYONE NEEDS TO KNOW®

TODD SANDLER

OXFORD
UNIVERSITY PRESS

5083

OXFORD
UNIVERSITY PRESS

Oxford University Press is a department of the University of Oxford. It furthers
the University's objective of excellence in research, scholarship, and education
by publishing worldwide. Oxford is a registered trade mark of Oxford University
Press in the UK and certain other countries.

"What Everyone Needs to Know" is a registered trademark
of Oxford University Press.

Published in the United States of America by Oxford University Press
198 Madison Avenue, New York, NY 10016, United States of America.

© Oxford University Press 2018

Library of Congress Cataloging-in-Publication Data
Names: Sandler, Todd, author.
Title: Terrorism: what everyone needs to know / Todd Sandler.
Description: New York : Oxford University Press, [2018] |
Includes bibliographical references and index.
Identifiers: LCCN 2017058668 (print) | LCCN 2018000428 (ebook) |
ISBN 9780190845865 (updf) | ISBN 9780190845872 (epub) |
ISBN 9780190845858 (pbk.) | ISBN 9780190845841 (hardcover)
Subjects: LCSH: Terrorism. | Terrorism—Prevention.
Classification: LCC HV6431 (ebook) | LCC HV6431.S2553 2018 (print) |
DDC 363.325—dc23
LC record available at https://lccn.loc.gov/2017058668

1 3 5 7 9 8 6 4 2
Paperback printed by LSC Communications, United States of America
Hardback printed by Bridgeport National Bindery, Inc., United States of America

To Tristan

CONTENTS

2 Causes of Terrorism   24

3 Role of Terrorist Groups   46

4 Effectiveness of Counterterrorism 70

5 Asymmetries and Terrorism 93

PREFACE

On a clear, bright morning on July 7, 2005, at 9:40 a.m., my wife and I stepped out of our hotel on Montague Street, London, to make our way to Russell Square Tube station to catch a train. The day before I had purchased higher-priced Underground passes that would have allowed us to take a train before 9:00 a.m., so that we could get an early start. This plan went awry when my wife decided to take a shower and start the day later than planned. Well, it was our summer holiday. As we reached Russell Square, there was a deafening blast, which was the suicide-bomb blast on a double-decker bus at Tavistock Place, a few blocks away, that killed thirteen people. The usual tranquil Russell Square was a scene of bedlam with police cars speeding through the park, police shouting at us to get away, and emergency vehicles everywhere outside the park's wrought iron fence. As we emerged from the square's exit nearest to the Tube stop, we saw dazed people, some with soot-covered faces, exiting the underground station.

Many thoughts flooded my mind: This is the face of terrorism! These stunned people could have been us, since the train coming from Kings Cross to Russell Square, which exploded between stations at 8:50 a.m., was the one that we had planned to take the day before. Although we would not have been on the train had we stuck to our original plan, we would have been on the platform to experience the sound of the blast, the screams of the victims, and the smoke filling the tunnel. To escape the smoke, we would have had to walk up the 171 steps of the spiral staircase of one of the deepest stations on the London Underground. Opened in 1906, almost a hundred years before, Russell Square Station does not have escalators, and the lifts would not have been advisable to take in such an emergency. I also thought that I never wanted to get so close to my research again! This frightening experience taught me that terrorism can touch anyone—me included—even though the likelihood of being touched is minuscule.

Even prior to the unprecedented hijackings on September 11, 2001 (henceforth, 9/11) that killed almost three thousand people and injured over twice that number, the world was acutely aware of the threat that terrorism posed. A few past watershed terrorist incidents include the US Marines barracks bombing in Beirut, Lebanon, on October 23, 1983; the downing of Air India Boeing 747 en route from Montreal to London on June 23, 1985; the downing of Pan Am Flight 103 en route from London to New York on December 21, 1988; the simultaneous bombings of the US embassies in Nairobi and Dar es Salaam on August 7, 1998; and the commuter train bombings in Madrid on March 11, 2004. Although watershed incidents generally result in large casualty tolls (deaths and injuries), most terrorist incidents kill and maim relatively few. The peak of transnational terrorism, which affects people or property from two or more countries, took place during 1980–1991, when the annual average number of attacks was 467. As religious fundamentalist terrorist groups replaced leftist terrorist groups as the dominant transnational terrorist influence in the late 1990s, the annual count of transnational terrorist attacks dropped drastically, but each attack involved greater carnage than in the earlier decades.

Currently, terrorism poses an ever-present threat that captures headlines and occupies our consciousness. Recent noteworthy attacks include truck massacres in Nice on Bastille Day on July 14, 2016, in Berlin at a Christmas market on December 19, 2016, and in Stockholm on Drottninggatan (a pedestrian street) on April 8, 2017. Other ghastly terrorist events include the Brussels airport and Maalbeek metro station suicide bombings on March 22, 2016, and the Atatürk Airport armed attack and suicide bombings on June 28, 2016. In the United States, recent terrorist attacks include the San Bernardino Inland Regional Center shooting that killed fourteen people on December 2, 2015, and the Orlando nightclub shooting that killed forty-nine people on June 12, 2016. Both shootings were ISIS-inspired, demonstrating the escalating concern of lone wolf terrorism. On October 31, 2017, Sayfullo Habibullaevich Saipov, a lone wolf terrorist, rammed a rental truck into cyclists and runners on the Hudson River Park's bike path in New York City. The attack killed eight and injured eleven.

Since 9/11, the threat of terrorism has directly affected our lives. Tens of billions of dollars are spent to support the US Department of Homeland Security (DHS), in which approximately two-thirds of its $66.8 billion budget in 2017 goes to addressing the terrorism threat. In addition, huge amounts of money are spent by the Federal Bureau of Investigation, the Central Intelligence Agency, and the US Department of Defense to address the terrorism threat. Other targeted countries also allocate large sums of money to protect against terrorist attacks. Our routines at airports were forever altered by 9/11 and subsequent terrorist incidents (for example, Richard Reed, "the shoe bomber," on December 22, 2001). The 9/11 attacks had a profound effect on the insurance premiums for buildings in major cities. The erection of barricades in front of federal buildings is another instance, where the risk of terrorism has impacted our lives. In this case, it was the bombing of the Alfred P. Murrah Federal Building in Oklahoma City on April 19, 1995, that created the need for novel security measures and new federal building designs. Incidents around the globe, reported on the news, remind us daily that terrorism remains a pertinent concern. As such, terrorism worries may influence our travel and vacation plans. Despite all of the expenditures on counterterrorism, American polls identified terrorism as the primary security concern prior to the 2016 presidential election. Populist candidates in the United States and Europe use the terrorist threat as an argument for restricting immigration.

The purpose of this book is to educate and demystify terrorism and its myriad aspects for readers that include college students, adult professionals, college-educated individuals, journalists, retirees, officeholders, and just about anyone who seeks a better understanding of modern-day terrorism. In a question-and-answer format, this book provides an informed analysis, free from ideology or politics, of the concept of terrorism, the causes of terrorism, the role of terrorist groups, the effectiveness of counterterrorism, asymmetries of terrorism, the economic consequences of terrorism, and the future of terrorism. I show that there are a lot of misconceptions about terrorism that have been inadvertently generated by the news media or elected officials. To accomplish this intended task, I draw on the findings from a large body of literature from political science, economics, and related disciplines. Articles in this literature base their conclusions on theoretical constructs that are tested with sophisticated empirical methods applied to real-world data on past terrorist incidents, influences, and observations. I conduct my questions and answers relatively free from jargon and technical terms to make my points accessible to a wide readership. I also aim to make the book interesting, provocative, and rather surprising in places.

To engage the reader's interests, I refer to key terrorist incidents throughout the book. These incidents are chosen to illustrate and highlight points being made in the text. There are literally thousands of incidents that can be chosen; however, most attacks are minor bombings or threats that are of little illustrative importance. Thus, I choose watershed events that the reader probably was aware of when they occurred. For instance, 9/11 changed airport security drastically, while the 1983 suicide bombing of the US Marines barracks in Beirut demonstrated that such bombings could result in concessions. The facts in the incidents are checked from trusted sources. At times, final casualty tolls may differ among sources, so that I rely on sources that update their tolls as new information becomes known. These sources are given in the notes.

I have researched terrorism for thirty-six years, well before interest in the topic grew after 9/11. My early contributions appeared in the *American Political Science Review, American Economic Review,* and the *Journal of Law and Economics,* all of which are premier journals. Early on, I worked with Edward Mickolus, Peter Flemming, and Jean Murdock (my wife) to put together a data set on transnational terrorist incidents that has been used by researchers for over thirty years. I have published articles on negotiations with terrorists, the economic consequences of terrorism, causes of terrorism, survival of terrorist groups, the effectiveness of counterterrorism, the role of international cooperation, and many other aspects of terrorism. I was a pioneer in applying game theory and other theoretic tools to the study of terrorism. For a ten-year period, I received grants from the US DHS to study various aspects of terrorism. I have talked with government officials and people at multilateral organizations (including Interpol and the United Nations) about my research findings on terrorism. I coauthored (with Walter Enders) *The Political Economy of Terrorism* (Cambridge University Press), now in its second edition. I have studied terrorism from many alternative vantage points. Finally, I have taught classes on terrorism for two decades. It is my hope that my varied experience allows me to write an informed, engaging, and useful book on a topic of significant importance.

ACKNOWLEDGMENTS

My greatest debt of gratitude is to my wife, Jeannie Murdock, who supported this project in so many ways. She typed the manuscript and provided helpful feedback throughout the process. She also gave me encouragement and was understanding as I focused so many hours on the manuscript. I also gratefully profited from comments offered by Carol Sandler, who read a draft of the manuscript. Her comments and encouragement are greatly appreciated. I also thank Dave McBride and David Pervin, senior editors at Oxford University Press (OUP), for their advice, comments, and belief in the project. I also thank Scott Parris, retired economics editor at OUP, for encouraging me to write a more general interest book. Two anonymous readers provided helpful comments on the proposed book. I also sent chapters to scholars, such as Wolfgang Buchholz, for their insights. I greatly profited from their feedback.

I also want to thank my many coauthors whom I have collaborated with on research articles on terrorism over the last thirty-six years. This collaboration played a large role in the genesis of this book. In particular, I want to thank Walter Enders and Khusrav Gaibulloev, from whom I have learned so much. My first articles on terrorism were written with Jon Cauley, Scott Atkinson, and John Tschirhart, all of whom stimulated my interest in applying economic reasoning to the study of terrorism. In addition, I thank Daniel Arce, Subhayu

Bandyopadhyay, Patrick Brandt, Javier Gardeazabal, Justin George, Kate Ivanova, Charlinda Jordan, Harvey Lapan, Raechelle Mascarenhas, James Piazza, Kevin Siqueira, Donggyu Sul, Javed Younas, and others.

Finally, I want to thank the many people at OUP who transformed the typescript into the printed book.

TERRORISM

WHAT EVERYONE NEEDS TO KNOW®

1

A PRIMER ON TERRORISM

What Is Terrorism?

Terrorism is the premeditated use or threat to use violence by individuals or subnational groups against noncombatants to obtain a political objective through the intimidation of a large audience beyond that of the immediate victims.[1] Two key ingredients in this definition are violence and the pursuit of a political goal. Violence, merely applied to extort money or to harm people or property without political ends, is a crime but not terrorism. Thus, kidnappings for ransoms that are not subsequently earmarked to support a political cause are not terrorism. In contrast, kidnappings by the Islamic State of Iraq and Syria (ISIS) are terrorist acts that not only advertise the group's goal to establish a caliphate in the region, but also fund its terrorist campaign.

In the standard definition, victims involve noncombatants, which include government officials, business people, private parties, and passive military individuals. Another important feature of the definition is the identification of the perpetrators as individuals or subnational groups. Individual perpetrators are known as lone wolf terrorists, while subnational group perpetrators are known as terrorist organizations. The latter includes al-Qaeda in Afghanistan, Boko Haram in Nigeria, al-Qaeda in the Islamic Maghreb (AQIM), Popular Front for the Liberation of Palestine (PFLP), ISIS, Abu Sayyaf in the Philippines, and Lashkar-e-Taiba in Pakistan. The above definition of terrorism rules out state terror as applied by Stalin and other dictators to control their own citizens. States can, however, support these subnational terrorist groups by providing safe havens, funding, intelligence, weapons, training, or other forms of assistance. Such support results in state-sponsored terrorism, as was the case of Libyan support for the downing of Pan Am Flight 103 over Lockerbie, Scotland, on December 21, 1988.[2] In 2003, Libya accepted responsibility and agreed to compensate the families of the victims of Flight 103. Definitions of terrorism allow for state sponsorship. In the 1980s, large-scale state-sponsored terrorist attacks were common, some of which were perpetrated by the Abu Nidal Organization (ANO). ANO carried out the infamous simultaneous armed attacks on the Rome and Vienna airports on December 27, 1985, that murdered 19 and injured 138. During its reign of terror, ANO amassed hundreds of millions of dollars as a terrorist group for hire.[3] It also assassinated many members of the rival Fatah group, founded by Yasser Arafat.

Another element of the definition of terrorism concerns the audience that terrorists seek to influence through the brutality of their violence. By trying to make their violence seem random, terrorists create a general atmosphere of anxiety wherein everyone feels at risk. As this atmosphere becomes more pervasive, citizens may press their government to reach some kind of accommodation with the terrorists even if it means making important policy changes. Liberal democracies that maintain their legitimacy by protecting lives and property are more vulnerable than autocracies to these citizen-generated pressures for tranquility.

What Tactics Are Used by Terrorists?

Terrorists employ many modes of attack to generate an atmosphere of fear. Their favorite attack mode consists of bombings that can assume various forms: explosive, letter, incendiary, car, or suicide bombings. The latter has become more popular after the 1990s and kills up to twelve people on average, compared to a conventional bombing that kills one on average.[4] Hostage-taking incidents, which are headline grabbers, include kidnappings, skyjackings, barricade and hostage taking (henceforth, barricade missions), and nonaerial hijackings of trains, buses, and ships. Barricade missions, where hostages are held in a building or location known to the authorities, were more popular during the 1970s and 1980s and included the takeover of the US Embassy in Tehran on November 4, 1979, by student extremists that lasted 444 days and likely cost Jimmy Carter the presidency. Kidnappings differ from the other three kinds of hostage events, since the hostages are secured in a location that is generally unknown to the authorities, thereby making kidnappings less risky and much longer in duration than the other kinds of hostage incidents.[5] As sources of funding for terrorists have been cut since 9/11, terrorists have resorted to more hostage taking, especially kidnappings, to make up for funding shortfalls. Other modes of terrorist attacks are assassinations, armed attacks, threats, and hoaxes.[6]

Figure 1.1 breaks down the number of transnational hostage-taking incidents into kidnappings, skyjackings, and others for 1968–2015.[7] Except for a few years (for example, 1980 and 1990), kidnapping represents the most frequent type of hostage incident. Both skyjackings and other kinds of hostage incidents (primarily barricade missions) declined greatly in numbers after 2001 owing to airport security enhancements and building hardening, respectively. These reactions provide evidence that terrorists respond rationally to elevated risk as they choose their portfolio of attacks. This strategic portfolio choice is analogous to the play choices made by sports teams. For example, a football team that excels in passing will still rush on occasions in order to keep its opponents guessing. Similarly, terrorist groups mix their modes of attacks to keep authorities

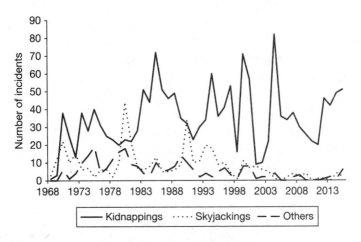

Figure 1.1 Transnational hostage-taking incidents, 1968–2015

off balance. This mixing of actions is a game-theoretic notion. Such notions also influence terrorists' choices—that is, greater security at airports after 9/11 resulted in terrorists turning to other types of less-protected hostage-taking events, such as kidnappings, as becomes clear in Figure 1.1. Throughout this book, we encounter strategic responses by the three main stakeholders of terrorism—the victims, the perpetrators, and the governments. As explained later, game theory has a huge role to play in fostering our understanding of terrorism and counterterrorism.

How Does Transnational Terrorism Differ from Domestic Terrorism?

Through the perpetrators, victims, or venue country, transnational or international terrorist incidents affect two or more countries. A terrorist attack on Westminster Bridge in London on March 22, 2017, that murdered an American tourist, among others, was a transnational terrorist incident, as were the terrorist attacks in Paris on November 13, 2015, perpetrated by ISIS terrorists who crossed into France from Belgium. Skyjackings that start in one country but conclude in a second country, such as skyjackings from various East Coast US cities to Cuba in the early 1980s, are transnational terrorist incidents, as are the skyjackings of domestic flights with some foreigners aboard. ISIS kidnappings of Americans and Europeans in Syria in 2013 and 2014 were also transnational terrorist attacks. Of course, the four hijackings on 9/11 constituted transnational terrorist incidents, because the dead and injured included over sixty nationalities.[8]

By contrast, domestic terrorism is homegrown and home-directed. As such, the victims and perpetrators are citizens of the venue country, where the attack takes place. The bombing of the Alfred P. Murrah Federal Building in Oklahoma City by Timothy McVeigh on April 19, 1995, was a domestic terrorist incident. The Unabomber's (Ted Kaczynski) package bombing campaign against US universities and airline companies during 1978–1995 consisted of domestic terrorist attacks. During the Vietnam War, there were many domestic terrorist bombings on US college campuses as a protest against US involvement in the war.

Domestic terrorist attacks have consequences for just the host or venue country, its institutions, citizens, property, and policies. These attacks are solely intended to reach and sway a domestic audience to bring about changes in domestic policies. For transnational terrorism, the audience is international as terrorists seek to influence another country's domestic or foreign policies or two or more countries' policies. Osama bin Laden's original demand for the United States to leave Saudi Arabia and more generally the Persian Gulf region resulted in US-targeted terrorist attacks in the region and elsewhere by al-Qaeda. Some transnational terrorist attacks are leveled against multilateral organizations, such as the Canal Hotel bombing in Baghdad, Iraq, on August 19, 2003. At the time, this hotel served as a regional headquarters for the United Nations.

Victims of the blast included Sérgio Vieira de Mello, the UN special representative in Iraq.

I shall later show that domestic terrorist incidents far out-number transnational terrorist incidents. Nonetheless, these latter incidents weigh more heavily on the minds of people in industrial countries for a number of reasons. First, trans-national terrorism generally exerts a greater influence than domestic terrorism on the economy in countries experiencing both kinds of terrorism. Second, by its nature, transna-tional terrorism has implications that transcend borders. Consequently, these attacks capture greater media attention than domestic terrorist attacks, especially beyond the venue country where the attack occurs. Third, transnational terrorist incidents are perpetrated by groups that pose threats to many countries, creating a need for coordination of counterter-rorism policies that is often difficult to achieve. Sovereign governments are loath to sacrifice their autonomy over secu-rity matters. By contrast, domestic terrorism poses a localized threat that can be addressed by the impacted nation's central government. Fourth, transnational terrorism can have secu-rity ramifications worldwide.[9] Fifth, transnational terrorism is much more costly to control because a targeted country must project its security forces to terrorist safe havens in distant host countries.

Why Should We Be Concerned about Terrorism?

Terrorism may change liberal democracies in profound ways by employing violence and its threat as a way to circumvent normal democratic processes. Terrorists make their demands for political change directly to elected officials. When these officials concede to such demands, democracy loses its power of majority rule as a small, violent minority effects a policy change. When political concessions are granted, the govern-ment is sending a clear signal to other minorities that terrorism may work. The granting of concessions may also result in backlash violence as the majority seeks to reverse the policy change.

Concerns over terrorism also arise because society must allocate huge amounts of resources to defend against it. From 2003 through 2011, the US Department of Homeland Security (DHS) budget rose by over 80 percent, or by almost 9 percent per year when averaged over the entire period. Currently, the DHS budget is about $67 billion, of which about two-thirds goes to protecting against terrorism.[10] The US Department of Defense also spends large amounts of money to fight ISIS and al-Qaeda in Iraq, Syria, Yemen, Afghanistan, and elsewhere. The Federal Bureau of Investigation and the Central Intelligence Agency also spend sizable amounts in countering terrorism. Even at the local level, police must secure public events against the threat of terrorism. Police efforts are now made more difficult with ISIS-inspired use of trucks to plow down people in public places. Since terrorists can attack almost anywhere, authorities must judiciously assign their resources based on a target's vulnerability, its value, and its likelihood of attack. In short, terrorism is a drain of government resources, and not every potential target can be protected.

Throughout the world, other countries must also spend on defensive and offensive measures to counter terrorism to keep their citizens safe. To guard against foreign terrorists, targeted countries must not only protect their borders and ports of entry, but must, at times, provide assistance to host countries to eradicate resident terrorist groups that attack these targeted countries' interests. Following 9/11, the United States increased its aid to countries with terrorist groups hostile to US interests. Such counterterrorism aid flows also characterized other industrial countries.[11]

Another reason for concern involves the rising carnage. Before 1990, leftist and nationalist/separatist terrorists were the dominant terrorist groups. From the early 1990s on, religious fundamentalist terrorist groups rose in prominence and were much more interested in killing and maiming victims. In terms of transnational terrorist attacks, 26 percent of incidents resulted in casualties (deaths or injuries) during 1968–1992, while 48 percent of incidents resulted in casualties during 1993–2015.[12] Another concern hinges on the recent rising number of transnational and domestic terrorist incidents, documented later in this chapter.

How Likely Are You to Be a Victim of a Terrorist Attack?

The simple answer is not very likely! One analyst characterizes the likelihood of an American being the victim of a transnational terrorist incident as less than the likelihood of being struck by lightning.[13] I can come up with an approximate probability of being a victim by looking at the data on transnational terrorist attacks over 2011–2015, when the annual average number of attacks is about 194 incidents. During this same period, US population averaged 316.5 million persons. If I assume that all transnational terrorist incidents involve Americans, then the likelihood of an American being in an incident is 6.13 chances out of ten million, or not very likely. Because each incident involved almost four deaths and six injuries, or ten casualties in total, the chances of being an American victim under this assumption increase to 6.13 out of one million adjusting for an incident having multiple victims. The chances of being struck by lightning in the United States is put at 1 in 960,000, so that my calculations put the chances of being a US victim of transnational terrorism at about six times that of being struck by lightning. Still, the chances of being a victim of terrorism are reassuringly low. It is, however, *much smaller* because in fact only about 18 percent of such incidents involved Americans during 2011–2015. Thus, we are back to the likelihood of being struck by lightning, about one in a million, as the likelihood of an American being a victim in a transnational terrorist incident!

Thus, one must wonder why so much money is allocated to counter terrorism if the risks appear to be relatively small. This hinges on an interesting counterfactual—what would the risks be if the United States and other targeted countries drastically reduced their counterterrorism expenditures? Obviously, the risks would be much greater as terrorists came to realize that it is much easier to engage in terrorist attacks. Elected officials do not want large-scale terrorist attacks on their watch; hence, they are apt to err on the side of caution when addressing terrorism. As a consequence, there is a proclivity to overspend on defensive measures against terrorism.[14] The horrific events on 9/11 show that the right terrorist attack can be devastating in terms of lives, limbs, and cost. If counterterrorism resources are properly spent, then high-valued targets are protected, shunting terrorists to low-valued ones. Counterterrorism actions also limit damages in the event of a successful attack and speed recovery in its aftermath.

What Is the Difference between Terrorism and Other Forms of Political Violence?

Political violence comes in forms other than terrorism. For example, an insurrection is an uprising of the people to overthrow the ruling government in the hopes of achieving a "fairer" or different distribution of income. Such insurrections are a likely reaction to a government that takes the lion's share of the wealth for itself. Unlike terrorism, insurrections involve a large portion of the populace that supports rebel leaders. By contrast, guerrilla warfare and terrorism are *tactics* that may be employed by rebel forces against the government. Guerrilla warfare is applied by mobile rebel forces to engage superior government military forces; terrorism is applied by subnational groups or individuals against government officials, police, and the public at large.

Civil or intrastate wars involve an armed conflict between a sovereign state and one or more organized subnational groups. In the ongoing Syrian Civil War, these groups include many rebel groups with different goals. At times, civil wars may include a third-party intervention, which may be another sovereign government. Russia, the United States, and France have intervened in the Syrian Civil War for or against the government or one of the rebel groups. At times, terrorism may be employed by rebels prior to, during, or after a civil war. The terrorism tactic may, but need not, be associated with a civil war. Most often, terrorism is applied in the absence of a civil war. For example, Italian Red Brigades, Action Direct, 17 November, Euskadi Ta Askatasuna (ETA), and Shining Path sought political goals without participating in a civil war. When terrorist groups control territory, they are more likely to resort to large-scale guerrilla warfare against government forces. As such, these land-controlling terrorist groups may become embroiled in a civil war.[15]

In general, terrorism can be treated as a tactical choice in civil wars and insurrections. However, terrorism usually exists without being tied to these conflicts.

Is Terrorism a New Phenomenon?

Terrorism has been around since the start of recorded history. For instance, the Zealots-Sicarii were Jewish terrorists who waged a terrorist campaign against the Romans who occupied Judea during the start of the first century. These terrorists also turned their attacks on compliant Jews and on the large Greek population in Judea. In many instances, Zealots employed a dagger to assassinate an intended victim. Zealots aimed to cause an insurrection against the Romans. Actually, their rather short-lived campaign of terror (66–73 CE) ended horribly for them with their temple destroyed and a mass suicide. A second important historic terrorist group was the Assassins, who carried on their terrorist campaign in Persia during 1090–1275 CE. Their political goal was to purify Islam by assassinating high-profile infidels. The Assassins were Shiites whose alleged enemies included prominent Sunni figures, among others.

Their terrorist campaign possessed many of the hallmarks of today's terrorism: transnational attacks, state sponsorship, and a religious base. In fact most terrorism before the nineteenth century was religion-based.[16]

Centuries later, the Boston Tea Party was probably the first prominent terrorist incident in the American colonies. This defiant act and others that followed initiated an insurrection that eventually resulted in the birth of the United States. The terrorism that founded the United States is best characterized as nationalist/separatist.

In more recent times, US terrorism dates back to attacks by anarchists who sought government-less rule in the late 1880s and the early part of the twentieth century. On September 6, 1901, President William K. McKinley was assassinated on the grounds of the Pan-American Exposition in Buffalo, New York, by Leon Czolgosz, an anarchist, whose attack mimicked the assassination of some European political figures by anarchists. In this regard, Czolgosz's act could be considered an anarchist-inspired attack well before the advent of satellite news coverage and the Internet. The assassination of President McKinley resulted in an act of Congress that provided Secret Service coverage for future US presidents.[17]

The largest terrorist bombing on US soil prior to the Oklahoma City bombing of the Alfred P. Murrah Federal Building in April 1995 was an anarchist-perpetrated bombing on Wall Street, New York City, on September 16, 1920, that killed thirty-eight and injured hundreds of people, 143 seriously. The one-hundred-pound dynamite bomb, detonated by a timing device, was in a horse-drawn wagon that carried five hundred pounds of iron sash weights, meant to inflict maximum casualties. Although automobiles have replaced wagons to transport bombs in most countries, this deadly attack shows that many things have remained the same over the last one hundred years.[18]

How Has Terrorism Changed since 1878 and the Rise of the Anarchists?

The recent era of transnational terrorism starting in 1878 is divided into four waves of overlapping terrorist campaigns. During each of these waves, one type of terrorist goal dominated; however, this is *not to imply* that other terrorist aims disappeared during each of the waves.[19] In fact, the four types of terrorist motivations coexisted during each wave, but in different proportions.

The first wave started in the late 1800s and ended at the beginning of World War I. This wave included the anarchists, whose People's Will group carried out the assassination of Czar Alexander II, along with a bombing campaign during 1878–1881. Anarchists wanted to replace established governments with people governance. They had a few notable achievements. First, they were the forerunner of the Russian Revolution, which brought the Communists to power. Second, they exported their terrorism internationally and stimulated assassinations of important political figures elsewhere, including President William McKinley. Third, they marked the start of modern-day transnational terrorism that transcends national borders.

The second wave consisted of the anticolonialists in the 1950s and 1960s, who were nationalist/separatist terrorists that pushed for independent states. Noteworthy campaigns included the Front de Libération Nationale's (FLN's) successful campaign against French rule in Algeria and the Zionists' successful campaign against British rule in Palestine. Even before these campaigns, the Irish Republican Army (IRA), led by Michael Collins, obtained Ireland's independence from Great Britain. Clearly, some nationalist/separatist terrorist campaigns have been successful.

The so-called third wave of leftist terrorists began in the late 1960s and continued into the early 1990s. This wave concluded with the breakdown of communism and the end of the Soviet Union's state sponsorship of some leftist terrorist groups. Marxism became less fashionable after the fall of many Eastern European Communist regimes. In response, some groups, such as the Red Army Faction in Germany, disbanded. Additionally, Western European countries launched an effective offensive against some left-wing terrorist groups. During their heyday, leftist terrorists were extremely active in Western Europe, Latin America, and North America. Even today, there are many leftist terrorist groups throughout the world.[20]

Religious fundamentalist terrorism constitutes the fourth wave. Although there were some notable fundamentalist attacks in the late 1970s and 1980s, the wave really got going in the 1990s with the rise of al-Qaeda and its network of associated groups. The first really significant fundamentalist attack was in November 1979 with the takeover of the US Embassy in Tehran, Iran. By the late 1990s, the religious fundamentalist terrorist attacks dominated those of the leftist and nationalist/ separatist terrorist groups in terms of the number and severity of terrorist attacks. With the rise of ISIS, Boko Haram, al-Shabaab, AQIM, al-Qaeda in the Arabian Peninsula, and many others, this dominance and its associated threats continue to grow today.

Despite these so-called waves, terrorists borrowed from their predecessors and, in so doing, perfected their methods. Terrorists paid heed to other groups' innovations even when they were on opposing sides. The Zionists borrowed from and improved on the terrorist tactics of Michael Collins and the IRA, and subsequently the Palestinian terrorists applied Zionists' terrorist tactics against the Israelis. Early on, terrorists favored urban centers for their attacks in order to capture maximum media attention and create great anxiety. Each wave of terrorism informed the next. Hezbollah's use of suicide attacks spread to the Tamil Tigers in Sri Lanka and then back to Hamas in Israel.

How Has Terrorism Changed since 1968?

Transnational terrorism really captured the world's attention with the hijacking by three PFLP terrorists of an El Al Airlines flight on July 22, 1968, en route from Rome to Tel Aviv. This incident lasted for forty days, until the last Israeli passengers were released. The hijacking garnered lots of media coverage and ended with the negotiated release by Israel of sixteen Arab prisoners from the 1967 Six Day War. Notably, the Israelis were forced to negotiate with the Palestinians—something that the Israelis had previously vowed never to do. The hijackers went free following the incident. This incident demonstrated that well-orchestrated skyjackings could have huge returns.[21] Many skyjackings followed, as is evident in Figure 1.1. To heighten the drama and gain a bargaining advantage, skyjackers sometimes killed a passenger early in the incident to show that they meant business and raise pressure on the government. Over time, skyjackers targeted flights with more passengers since that raised the cost to the government from not reaching a negotiated concession with the terrorists.

To provide a perspective on terrorism during the last half-century, I begin with a plot of all transnational terrorist attacks for 1968–2015 (Figure 1.2). A number of features are evident. First, the peak of such attacks came during the 1970s and 1980s, when these attacks averaged around 413 incidents per year. Second, terrorist attacks are cyclical, with peaks and troughs; hence, a downturn is no reason for rejoicing! Third, since the early 1990s and the emerging dominance of the religious fundamentalist terrorists, transnational terrorist attacks now average 178 incidents a year, or 43 percent of the attacks during the third-wave era. This is not all good news since I shall shortly show that incidents' casualties increased in recent years. Fourth, there is a clear uptick in the number of incidents since 2011. Even so, the media-generated impression that such attacks are more prevalent today than ever before is simply false.[22]

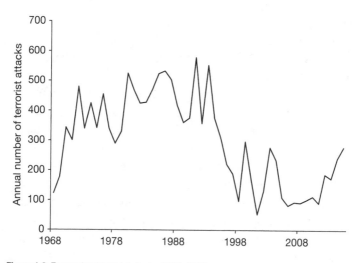

Figure 1.2 Transnational terrorist attacks, 1968–2015

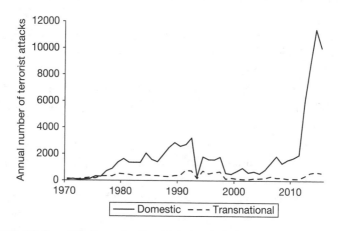

Figure 1.3 Domestic and transnational terrorist attacks, 1970–2015

Figure 1.3 displays the annual number of domestic terrorist attacks for 1970–2015, based on the Global Terrorism Database (GTD), which tracks both domestic and transnational terrorist attacks. For comparison purposes, the dashed path indicates the annual number of transnational terrorist attacks according to the GTD. The drop-off in 1993 is not due to some terrorist holiday but a lost year of data. Apparently, during an office move by Pinkerton Security, which originally collected the data, the box for 1993 fell off of the truck, never to be retrieved. In Figure 1.3, there are a number of noteworthy features. The scale on the vertical axis is in the thousands, while the scale on the vertical axis in Figure 1.2 for transnational terrorist attacks is in the hundreds. Thus, the yearly number of domestic terrorist attacks has far outnumbered that of transnational attacks since 1977, when the GTD better accounted for domestic terrorist incidents. There is an ominous rise in domestic terrorism starting in 2005 that exploded in 2013. Part of this recent spike is due to a change in the GTD coding practices, which now more generously count domestic events. These attacks are increasing, in part, because 9/11 made it more difficult for terrorists to cross national borders, so that more attacks occur at home in Africa, the Middle East, and Asia. Since domestic terrorism is not a large concern in most developed countries, many readers are unaware of its threat. This complacency is misguided because domestic terrorism can inhibit development, thereby limiting the effectiveness of foreign aid. In addition, domestic terrorism can morph into transnational terrorism.[23]

Figure 1.4 shows that the percentage of terrorist incidents ending in casualties is larger for domestic than for transnational terrorist attacks; however, this difference has been closing since 2009. Given the rising dominance of religious fundamentalist terrorists, there is an upward trend to the percentage of transnational terrorist incidents ending in casualties after 1999. Even though these terrorists conduct fewer attacks than their leftist counterparts, religious fundamentalist terrorists seek more casualties per incident. From 1970 to 1992, 340 people lost their lives annually in transnational terrorist attacks; from 1993 to 2010, 450 people lost their lives annually in transnational terrorist attacks, excluding 9/11. In comparison, between 30,000 and 40,000 die annually just on

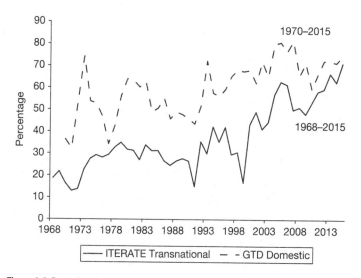

Figure 1.4 Proportion of domestic and transnational terrorist incidents with casualties

US highways. The deaths from 9/11 are purposely left out, but would increase the annual death toll from transnational terrorism during 1993–2010 to 606 persons. During 2011–2015, 749 people died annually in such terrorism. Nevertheless, it is surprising, and rather fortunate, how few people perish annually in transnational terrorist attacks worldwide.

Finally, I disaggregate these incident totals into their constituent classes of attack: bombings, hostage takings, armed attacks, assassinations, and other incidents (for example, sabotage, threats, and hoaxes) for two snapshots in time, 1968–2001 and 2002–2015. In Figure 1.5, percentages for 1968–2001 indicate that bombings are the most common type of transnational terrorist attack, followed by hostage takings, armed attacks, and assassinations. After 2001, the percentages of bombings and other incidents fell, while the percentages of hostage and armed attacks rose. Hostage taking, especially kidnappings, rose as terrorists sought alternative sources of funding after post-9/11 measures cut off many past funding sources. The increasing prevalence of armed attacks is due to religious

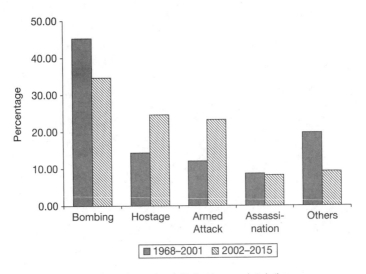

Figure 1.5 Transnational terrorism modes of attack at two snapshots in time

fundamentalist terrorists' liking for the spectacle of armed attacks in public places.

Figure 1.6 displays the percentage breakdown for domestic terrorist attacks. Bombings are a greater percentage of domestic attacks than of transnational attacks. Before 2002, the tiny percentage of hostage incidents is an artifice due to undercounting such incidents prior to the management of the data set by the University of Maryland. After 2002, there are percentage increases in bombings, hostage takings, and armed attacks, and percentage decreases in assassinations and other attacks. The latter incidents decrease in both Figures 1.5 and 1.6 due to reduced media coverage of threats and hoaxes following 9/11. Remember that these event data sets are compiled by researchers from media accounts. After 9/11, the media did not view victimless incidents as newsworthy, which partly explains the large decrease in transnational terrorism in Figure 1.2.

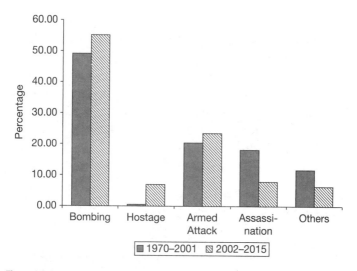

Figure 1.6 Domestic terrorism modes of attack at two snapshots in time

Are Terrorists Rational?

Most social scientists today view terrorists as rational individuals who attempt to maximize some payoff or goal subject to constraints. Their behavior is predictable to a degree—for example, if the authorities raise the price or difficulty of, say, skyjackings through airport metal detectors, then terrorists are anticipated to substitute now relatively cheaper kidnappings, not protected by metal detectors. This predictability does not mean that the authorities are able to know which potential kidnap victim will be taken. Only human intelligence can make this determination.

Rationality is not judged based on the desirability of terrorists' goals but on their ability to respond in an appropriate fashion to alterations in their constraints. To view terrorists as rational is not to condone their tactics or goals, which I emphatically do not. There is no justification or cause that warrants killing and maiming innocent people for a principle or political goal, no matter how noble. There are no "good terrorists"! Researchers' crusade to legitimize the study of terrorist rationality and, more generally, the application of science to identify effective counterterrorism measures has resulted in many innovative and important studies. Today, there are innumerable scholars and analysts who treat terrorists as rational actors. The DHS funds many Centers of Excellence to conduct such studies.

Why Is Game Theory an Appropriate Tool to Analyze Terrorism and Counterterrorism?

Game theory is the study of strategic rational choice. As such, game theory allows choices by agents or "players" (for example, terrorists, victims, or targeted governments) to be influenced by and responsive to the choices of others. Despite its name, game theory is not a frivolous method; rather, it is a highly rigorous methodology that draws from many branches of mathematics, including calculus, probability theory, statistics, real analysis, modern algebra, topology, graph theory, and dynamic optimization. Game theory was developed in secret during World War II as a means, among other things, to improve US pilots' ability to win dogfights with enemy fighter planes.

Game theory is an appropriate tool to study terrorism and the practice of counterterrorism because it fosters understanding of how adversaries (terrorists and a targeted government) and how allies (two or more commonly targeted governments or countries) choose their actions or *strategies*. Consider how two countries, both targeted by al-Qaeda, decide their defensive measures. For equal potential payoffs, the terrorists direct their attack against the softer target. If, for instance, French airports are more secure than those in Belgium, then al-Qaeda is more likely to hijack a plane departing from Belgium. In fact, countries may engage in a fortification race in the hopes of deflecting potential attacks abroad, where they possess fewer interests.[24] As a consequence, countries may overspend on defensive measures against terrorism.

Game theory allows players to make strategic moves in order to gain an advantage over their opponents. Thus, governments may pledge never to concede ransoms to terrorist kidnappers in the hopes of ending such kidnappings. If the would-be kidnappers believe the government's pledge, then there are no concessionary gains from abducting hostages. The trick is for the government to hold firm even when the hostage is particularly important or his or her life hangs in the balance. In recent years, the United States has maintained its pledge in some heartrending circumstances, while other European countries have not.

Game theory also permits learning as a player's past actions allow opponents or allies to update their view of that player's unobservable attributes. For example, a government may not know the resources or capabilities of a nascent terrorist group. As the government observes the group's campaign of terrorism over time, the government can update its assessment of the threat that the group poses and can choose its counterterrorism measures accordingly.[25]

Game theory stresses the strategic dynamics of terrorists and targeted governments. As will be shown throughout the book, game theory can provide counterintuitive insights that become understandable once the reactions of players are taken into account.

Why Is There a Need for Empirical Studies on Terrorism?

The scientific method involves formulating a theory that is subsequently tested empirically with unbiased data. If the empirical test supports the theory, then the theory is maintained for the time being until a better, more predictive theory is formulated. When the empirical test does not support the theory, a replacement theory is sought and then tested. I firmly believe that the study of terrorism and counterterrorism must be founded on this scientific paradigm and should not be based on ideology or casual empiricism. The latter derives from the support of an anecdotal case or two. Hence, throughout this book, I refer to rigorous empirical studies in the endnotes that back up my contentions. My confidence in the theory grows when multiple empirical tests, utilizing alternative methods, support it.

Is Terrorism Successful?

The success of terrorism is much debated among scholars. First and foremost, a definition of success is required. Terrorist groups' success can be tied to their ability to inflict damage and gain visibility for their cause. Alternatively, success can hinge on the groups' ability to secure some or all of their demands. The former is combat success and the latter is strategic success. I favor the more stringent strategic success as the preferred criterion, but caution that partial goal fulfillment should be viewed as a strategic success. When job candidates make salary demands, candidates typically ask for more than they need to take the job. If the candidates settle for less than their initial demands, their acceptance of the offer indicates a successful negotiation. Analogously, terrorist groups that end their campaign of terror when given some of their demands are viewed as strategically successful.

The American revolutionaries, the FLN, and the Zionists were fully successful in gaining independence for the United States, Algeria, and Israel, respectively. In 1984, Hezbollah was successful in forcing the US-led multinational force to leave Lebanon in the wake of its suicide bombings of the US Marines barracks and the French paratroopers sleeping quarters in Beirut on October 23, 1983. The evidence of strategic success is mixed. One scholar finds that six of eleven terrorist suicide bombing campaigns were successful in achieving some significant policy concessions. Another study of terrorist campaigns finds that only 7 percent of twenty-eight sample campaigns

achieved their stated demands. I am troubled by the question-
able representativeness of these small samples to allow for unbiased statistical inference. A recent study of over five hundred
terrorist groups finds that 23 percent either achieved victory
or joined the political process to pursue their goals. Although
the strategic success of terrorist groups is not large, it is by no
means nil. Studies show that nationalist/separatist groups are
more successful than religious fundamentalist, left-wing, and
right-wing groups. Moreover, keeping demands specific and
not grandiose favors strategic success (see chapter 3).[26]

2

CAUSES OF TERRORISM

What Are the Main Causes of Terrorism?

The four waves of terrorism, presented in chapter 1, demonstrate some general causes of terrorism: anarchy, nationalism, leftist ideology, and religious fundamentalism. This list is by no means exhaustive. At times, terrorism may be motivated by issue-specific political aims, such as promoting animal rights, ending the Vietnam War, reducing income inequality, ending apartheid, or eliminating abortions. At other times, economic discrimination against a specific ethnic group may motivate terrorism. The Protestant majority allegedly discriminated against the Catholics before and during the times of the "The Troubles," the political violence in Northern Ireland during 1968–1998. Such discrimination may result in humiliation and grievances that may erupt in violence. Some terrorist groups are right-wing extremists, who may engage in reactionary acts of intolerance and violence aimed at African Americans, Jews, Catholics, Muslims, and other groups. Other right-wing groups may use terrorism to pursue a nationalist campaign that often targets immigrants or federal officials. In some instances, a country's foreign policy may anger and induce citizens in other countries to direct their violence against the country's people and property abroad. Such attacks are known as transnational terrorism. In the 1970s, leftist terrorists planted bombs at US military bases and facilities in European cities to protest NATO or US troops stationed in Europe.[1]

Suffice it to say that terrorism has myriad root causes. In the aftermath of a momentous terrorist event, such as 9/11 or the Madrid commuter train bombings on March 11, 2004, political leaders and the media try to identify a single cause for such terrorist attacks. If, indeed, a single root cause could be distilled, then an effective counterterrorism strategy might be to address or lessen this motivating cause. Thus, on March 22, 2002, President George W. Bush said in a speech in Monterrey, Mexico, that "we fight against poverty because hope is an answer to terror."[2] As a consequence, President Bush redirected US aid to help fight the war on terror. Despite his speech, much of the increased aid went to bolster recipient countries' offensives against a resident terrorist threat that presented transnational terrorism risks to the United States. The aid did not necessarily go to alleviating poverty in the recipient country.[3]

The alleged link between poverty and terrorism is examined later in the chapter. Since President Bush's speech, many scholarly articles have investigated this link with very mixed results. There is a marked irony about using tied foreign aid to fight transnational terrorism on behalf of the United States. If unpopular foreign policy sparks transnational terrorism, as some scholars assert,[4] then US-tied aid can be a stimulus, rather than an inhibitor, of such attacks on US interests. Recipient regimes may be viewed by their citizens as US puppets, thereby encouraging terrorist attacks that increase local political instability, which ideally suits the resident terrorists. Additionally, grievances may follow if the aid skews the income distribution more in favor of the ruling class.

After 9/11, globalization was put forward as a cause of transnational terrorism. Globalization refers to augmented transactions of all types across international borders. These transactional flows include goods, services, financial capital, productive factors, foreign direct investment, diseases, ideas, and virtual transmissions. Two bouts of globalization have occurred since the late nineteenth century: from the late 1870s to the start of World War I, and from the latter half of the twentieth century until now. During the first era, there were unprecedented increases in trade and immigration flows. The former was encouraged by reduced trade barriers as tariffs fell precipitously. During the current era, trade and financial flows increased markedly; however, labor mobility is less than that of the first era of globalization. Both globalization eras are associated with increased transnational terrorism, perpetrated by the anarchists during the first era and by the anticolonialists, leftists, and religious fundamentalists during the second era.[5]

An essential message here is that terrorism, whether domestic or transnational, has no single or primary cause. Additionally, domestic terrorism may respond more fully to some motivating factors than does transnational terrorism, and vice versa. The relationship between terrorism and poverty, or between terrorism and globalization, is more nuanced than first believed after 9/11. Finding a simple cause is made more difficult because there often exist two-way relationships—for example, terrorism may influence average earnings per person, while the latter may affect terrorism. We often conceptualize the relationship between a cause and an effect as two things varying in a linear fashion, so that a unit increase in the cause results in a proportional response. However, the true relationship may be nonlinear or more involved.

Is Globalization a Cause of Transnational Terrorism?

At 5:30 a.m. on September 5, 1972, eight heavily armed Black September terrorists stormed the Israeli athletes' quarters at the Olympic Games in Munich, West Germany. In the ensuing struggle, two Israeli athletes were murdered, nine were taken hostage, and six escaped. After securing the nine hostages, the terrorists demanded the release of 236 Palestinian guerrillas from Israeli jails and five terrorists from West German prisons.

The latter included Andreas Baader and Ulrike Meinhof, two of the founding members of the Red Army Faction (RAF). Many hours of tense negotiations ensued, with the terrorists threatening to kill one or more hostages by set deadlines if their demands were not met. Repeatedly, these deadlines passed uneventfully. At 10:10 p.m. on the day of the abduction, the terrorists, accompanied by their hostages, boarded a bus that took them to two waiting helicopters, which then flew them to Fürstenfeldbruck Military Airport. Once at the airport, the terrorists and their hostages were scheduled to board a Lufthansa 727 aircraft to be flown to Egypt for an allegedly agreed-upon exchange of hostages. The plan went horribly wrong when West German marksmen opened fire on some of the Palestinian terrorists on the tarmac. In the following frantic moments, one terrorist lobbed a grenade into the helicopter containing the nine athletes, all of whom perished in the blast and subsequent fire.[6]

Satellite transmission of such sporting events provided a global audience for this terrorist incident. It is estimated that 900 million viewers from over a hundred countries watched the horrific events unfold live on their television screens. Even though the terrorists failed to secure any of their demands and five of the eight terrorists were killed at the airport, the incident made the Palestinian struggle known to the world. In the incident's aftermath, many young men joined Palestinian terrorist organizations.[7] Following this incident, the number of transnational terrorist incidents averaged 426 each year over the next sixteen years, compared to 237 each year during 1968–1971.

This incident illustrates how globalization, partly captured by advances in communication transmission, can be associated with more transnational terrorist attacks as terrorists seek a world stage to broadcast their grievances. Although such incidents indicate that there is an *association* between some aspects of globalization and transnational terrorism, these attacks do not necessarily establish that globalization *causes* such terrorism. To address the causal question, researchers must test one or more measures of globalization against a measure of transnational terrorism (for example, the number of incidents per year) to show that globalization explains changes in transnational terrorism when other potential causes are held constant.

When trade flows, portfolio investments, and foreign direct investments are used to measure economic globalization, no causal link is identified between these globalization measures and transnational terrorism. That is, countries displaying greater economic globalization in terms of more cross-border transactions did not sustain more transnational terrorist incidents. In a subsequent study that used an index of economic and political globalization (for example, membership in alliances or treaties) to capture countries' integration in the global community, no relationship between the globalization index and transnational terrorism was uncovered. In general, countries with a greater presence as global players did not necessarily attract more transnational terrorism.[8]

Does Poverty Cause Terrorism?

President Bush's remarks, cited earlier, about poverty being a cause of terrorism motivated much research on this alleged linkage.[9] In economics, the well-being of a country's citizens is measured by the country's income per capita or the average income earnings of its citizens. Low income per capita is equated with poverty, as the typical citizen has little to live on. For most countries, income per capita is reported on an annual basis.

To address the potential linkage between poverty and terrorism, a couple of studies rely on public opinion polls in the West Bank and Gaza Strip. These polls showed that a large majority of highly educated, and presumably wealthier, Palestinians supported the use of terrorism. Illiterate and poorer Palestinians displayed a much lower margin of support for terrorism than their richer and more-educated counterparts, thus suggesting no link between poverty and terrorism. An initial article on this alleged poverty-terrorism linkage also studies the background of Hezbollah fighters. Among such militants, the poverty rate was 28 percent, compared to 33 percent for the base Lebanese population. In this prominent study involving up to 148 countries, terrorists were not more likely to come from poorer countries when basic civil liberties (for example, freedom of association and protection of civil rights) are controlled in the analysis. That is, the lack of basic civil freedoms, and not poverty, appears to influence transnational terrorism.[10]

In numerous subsequent studies, economists and political scientists have investigated the relationship between domestic or transnational terrorism and income per capita. The results in these studies vary considerably, with some articles finding a positive linear relationship, others finding a negative linear relationship, and still others finding no relationship between income per capita and terrorism.[11] A negative linear relationship would imply that low income per capita or poverty causes a greater amount of terrorism, as thought by President Bush, media commentators, and others. Notably, many fewer studies uncover the negative relationship than those that uncover a positive or no relationship between income per capita and terrorism. A positive relationship would indicate that richer countries experience more terrorist attacks.

A recent study sorts out these various findings by establishing a robust hill-shaped relationship between income per capita and alternative forms of terrorism.[12] Such a hill-shaped relationship indicates that terrorism is greatest for some middle range of income per capita, so that neither poor nor really rich countries sustain very much domestic or transnational terrorism. The storyline behind these results is that people in really poor countries are more interested in their subsistence and focusing on surviving another day. Thus, they possess little means for supporting or engaging in terrorist campaigns at home or abroad. Some citizens in poor countries may have grievances, but they do not have the resources to act on them. By contrast, citizens in rich countries generally have few grievances that may erupt in domestic terrorism. Moreover, rich countries possess the means to crush domestic terrorism and to project power abroad to attack foreign-based terrorist groups. The US use of drone attacks on terrorist groups in Iraq, Pakistan, Syria, and Yemen is an apt example of power projection, as is the US dropping of a GBU-43/B Massive Ordinance Air Blast (MOAB) bomb on Islamic State in Iraq and Syria (ISIS) caves in Afghanistan on April 13, 2017. MOAB is a 21,600-pound bomb that is the largest nonnuclear bomb in the US arsenal.

In middle-income countries, terrorist groups can attract operatives to conduct terrorist attacks at home and abroad to make their grievances known and to issue demands for political change. Middle-income countries have fewer means than rich countries to counter terrorist threats. This is particularly true of actions to curb transnational terrorist attacks at home or against the countries' interests abroad. This hill-shaped relationship between income per capita and terrorism applies to the pre-1993 reign of the leftist terrorists and to the post-1993 reign of the religious fundamentalist terrorists. In the earlier period, the *peak* number of terrorist attacks is found to occur at a higher income per capita level than during the latter period. Leftist terrorists concentrated their attacks throughout Europe and Latin America, while religious fundamentalists focused their attacks in Africa, Asia, and the Middle East. Generally, leftist terrorist attacks took place in more well-to-do countries than the more recent terrorist attacks of the religious fundamentalists, except for the occasional attack in a European capital city. This hill-shaped relationship also applies to venue countries, which are the scene of the attack, and to perpetrator countries, which are the origin state of the terrorists. This recent finding indicates that terrorism is not motivated by poverty per se. Notably, the hill-shaped relationship between terrorist attacks and income per capita continues to hold when other considerations, such as income inequality, civil liberties, and population, are included.

What Is the Relationship between Terrorism and Education?

Terrorist leaders are intent on getting their missions completed as planned. In a study of suicide terrorism, Palestinian terrorist groups are found to assign more educated and older suicide bombers to the high-valued targets in large cities in order to wreak more carnage.[13] This is a rational use of resources since terrorist groups apparently have no trouble in attracting suicide bombers. Economists have taught us that education is the best screening device for hiring people that can accomplish tasks successfully. Apparently, suicide terrorism is no exception. Perhaps, counter to intuition, there is a high positive association between suicide terrorists and higher education. Consider Mohammed Atta, who crashed American Airlines Flight 11 into the North Tower of the World Trade Center on 9/11. Atta was from a prominent middle-class family in Egypt and had earned an architecture degree from the University of Cairo. He had also enrolled for an advanced degree in architecture from the Technical University of Hamburg. The other three pilots on 9/11—Khalid al-Mihdhar, Marwan al-Shehhi, and Ziad Jarrah—were from middle- to upper-class families and had attended various universities. Clearly, al-Qaeda picked pilots who could quickly master the requisite skills for flying the planes into the planned targets. Illiterate and poor operatives would not have been able to acquire such skills.

Is Income Inequality a Driver of Terrorism?

In a particular country, income inequality is measured by a Gini coefficient. A Gini coefficient of 0 indicates perfect equality: 1 percent of the families earn 1 percent of the country's income, 10 percent of the families earn 10 percent of the country's income, 20 percent of the families earn 20 percent of the country's income, and so on. In contrast, a Gini coefficient of 1 indicates complete inequality, in which a single family earns 100 percent of the country's income. As the Gini coefficient increases in value from 0, the country's income distribution becomes more unequal. When the Gini coefficient is used to explain terrorist attacks, there is frequently no relationship, so that income inequality is typically not viewed as a determinant of domestic or transnational terrorism.[14] This negative finding makes sense when one thinks back to the plot of transnational terrorist incidents in Figure 1.2 in chapter 1. Recall that the peak of this terrorism came during the late 1970s and 1980s. In more recent times, world income distribution has become more unequal, but transnational terrorist attacks have declined greatly in number. The plot of domestic terrorist attacks in Figure 1.3 in chapter 1 also does not track the worsening domestic income inequality over time. That is, there is no clear association between the number of domestic terrorist attacks and the worsening income inequality.

If, however, income inequalities stem from economic discrimination targeting a particular ethnic group, then domestic terrorism may result. Such discrimination breeds grievances that may generate terrorist attacks. An interesting study shows that countries with minority groups that experienced economic discrimination sustained more domestic terrorist incidents. These incidents were reduced in number when public policies were instituted to mitigate or protect against economic discrimination. Moreover, countries with no minority group economic discrimination had much less domestic terrorism. Notably, economic discrimination did not affect transnational terrorism, or attacks against other countries or their interests.[15] Apparently, economic discrimination results in attacks at home, directed against those engaging in the discrimination.

A more recent, and somewhat different, analysis focuses on religious discrimination possibly directed at over four hundred religious minorities in the developing world. Thus, unlike the previous study, this new study does not include minority groups in *both* developed and developing countries. Moreover, the new study's measure of political violence is an armed conflict and not terrorism per se. Armed conflicts imply much greater violence than terrorism. This study indicates that state-imposed religious discrimination resulted in grievances, but these grievances did not generally create armed conflicts.[16]

Has Religion Been a Driver of Terrorism since the Start of the 1990s?

At 8:22 a.m. on May 31, 2017, a massive suicide car bomb exploded near Zanbaq Square in the heart of the diplomatic quarter of Kabul. The bomb left a thirteen-foot-deep crater and extensively damaged the nearby German Embassy. Initially, more than 90 people were reported as killed and over 400 were injured. Sadly, the death toll was raised later to 150. The Taliban-claimed bombing was believed to have been done by the Haqqani Network, a Taliban-affiliated group. The incident was a transnational terrorist attack since foreign persons were killed or injured and foreign property damaged.[17] This bombing and countless others since the early 1990s can be traced to religious fundamentalist terrorism. Just the day prior to the Kabul bombing, an ISIS car bomb near an ice cream parlor in the center of Baghdad murdered seventeen people, including children, and injured thirty-two others. This attack was followed two hours later by a second explosion that killed fourteen people and injured thirty-four others outside a government pension office in Baghdad. Recently, ISIS has increased such heinous attacks with their indiscriminate carnage as it has lost hold of territory in Iraq.[18] Both the Taliban and ISIS are religious fundamentalist terrorist groups that seek territory in which they can impose their religious views on others. ISIS, a Sunni group, often targets Shiites.

Such attacks characterize the fourth wave of modern terrorism (see chapter 1), where religious fundamentalist terrorist attacks are prevalent. There are a number of noteworthy characteristics of religious fundamentalist terrorist attacks. First, these attacks aim for high casualties. Second, religious fundamentalist terrorists may deploy suicide bombers to raise body counts. Third, all nonbelievers are legitimate targets, including women and children. The horrific suicide bombing at the Manchester Arena in England on May 22, 2017, purposely targeted teenage and younger girls at an Ariana Grande concert. This attack killed 23 people and injured another 116; the attack illustrates these first three characteristics. Fourth, religious fundamentalist terrorists issue vague generalized threats, but do not give any advanced warnings. Fifth, these terrorists rely on bombings, armed attacks, and kidnappings. Sixth, they express an interest in engaging in chemical, biological, radiological, and nuclear terrorist attacks but, to date, have relied on more conventional means of attack.[19]

Certainly, over the last couple of decades, religion provided a motive for many terrorist attacks. As mentioned in chapter 1, religion was a motive for the Zealots-Sicarri uprising against the Roman occupation of Judea during the first century. Religion also offered a motive for the Assassins' attacks a thousand years later against non-Shia officials. Thus, religion has been a longtime cause of terrorism and continues to be a cause.

Are Domestic and Transnational Terrorism Driven by the Same Causes?

The previously mentioned study on economic discrimination indicates that domestic, but not transnational, terrorism increases as minority economic discrimination grows in importance at the country level. Thus, the simple answer to the question posed is that these two types of terrorism are not necessarily driven by the same causes. During the Vietnam War, there were many domestic terrorist incidents in the United States that protested this war. Anti-abortion bombings in the

United States are domestic terrorist attacks. In fact, many issue-specific terrorist attacks are domestic if the issue and the target concern just the host country.

At times, both types of terrorism may be driven by the same cause. In Greece during 1975–2002, the Revolutionary Organization of 17 November (better known as 17 November) assassinated twenty-three people and engaged in 103 terrorist attacks against American, British, Turkish, and Greek targets. The group protested a variety of foreign and domestic policies, including Greek membership in NATO, US presence in Europe, the practice of capitalism, and Greek deployment of security forces. On December 23, 1975, three gunmen from 17 November murdered Richard S. Welch, the Athens station chief of the Central Intelligence Agency at the time, as he and his wife returned from the US ambassador's Christmas party. This assassination was the initial terrorist attack by 17 November. On December 15, 1976, the group assassinated Evanghelos Mallios, the former intelligence chief of the Greek security police. The assassination of Welch was a transnational terrorist incident, while the assassination of Mallios was a domestic terrorist incident. Both attacks were motivated by the same cause—Greek policies. The 17 November reign of terror only ended in 2002 after the capture of Savas Xiros, a church icon painter, on June 29. Xiros lost his hand in a failed bomb attempt on the Flying Dolphins ferry company in Piraeus. From his hospital bed, the recovering terrorist provided the names of other group members, resulting in more arrests and the eventual capture of most, if not all, group members. The tightly knit structure of 17 November meant that the capture of even one member compromised the entire group (see chapters 3 and 5).[20]

Many of the European leftist terrorist groups engaged in both domestic and transnational terrorist attacks to protest their home country's domestic and foreign policies. Such groups included the Combatant Communist Cells (CCC), Direct Action (DA), First of October Anti-Fascists Resistance Group (GRAPO),

Popular Forces 25 April (FP-25), RAF, and Revolutionary Cells (RZ). For instance, GRAPO in Spain conducted a terrorist campaign during 1975–2007 that was driven by its anticapitalist and anti-imperialist views. The latter motive was fueled by anger over Spain's membership in NATO. Spain joined NATO on May 31, 1982, becoming the sixteenth member. GRAPO's anticapitalist agenda resulted in domestic and transnational terrorist attacks. At times, these transnational incidents were against foreign direct investment or foreign ownership and management of firms located in Spain.

Are Foreign Policy Decisions a Driver of Transnational Terrorism?

As in the case of the European leftist groups, some transnational terrorist attacks are motivated by foreign policy decisions. During 2016–2017, ISIS terrorist attacks in the United Kingdom and France were motivated, in large part, by these countries' bombing of ISIS assets in Syria and Iraq. Engaging in such aerial assaults on ISIS represents foreign policy decisions on the part of the United Kingdom and France. Since the targets of these ISIS-inspired or ISIS-directed terrorist attacks are foreigners, these attacks are necessarily transnational. On 9/11, al-Qaeda was protesting US presence in the Arabian Peninsula—a US foreign policy decision. To date, empirical studies have achieved mixed success in establishing foreign policy—even that of the United States—as a root cause of transnational terrorism for a large sample of countries.[21] It is easy to look at a specific transnational terrorist incident and tie it to the targeted country's foreign policy decisions. However, it is far more difficult to establish foreign policy as a primary driver of transnational terrorism *in general*. To establish this causation, a researcher must hold other potential causes of transnational terrorism constant and possess a sufficiently unbiased (randomly drawn) sample from which to draw a statistical inference.

The examination of a few cases that suggest a causal link between foreign policy decisions and transnational terrorism does not establish that there is a true causality that remains when other potential causes are controlled. A common mistake made by officeholders and the media is to jump from one or a few valid examples to a general causal statement. This temptation must be resisted if we are to understand the drivers of terrorism and, thus, what can be done to curb terrorism.

Does Immigration Foster Transnational Terrorism?

This is a question of significant political and policy importance. During his election campaign in 2016, Donald Trump linked potential terrorist attacks on US soil to Muslim immigration into America. After being elected president, President Trump imposed an immigration travel ban from seven, and later six, predominantly Muslim countries. A populist candidate in France in 2017 also alleged this link and used anti-immigration rhetoric to try to win office but, this ploy failed.

Four recent ISIS-inspired or ISIS-directed terrorist attacks suggest that the link is not as obvious as one may think. On July 14, 2016, Mohamed Lahouaiej-Bouhlel, a Tunisian immigrant, drove a truck into a crowd, observing a Bastille Day fireworks display along the Nice beachfront in France. The attack killed 86 people and injured 434. Just over five months later, on December 19, 2016, Anis Amri, a Tunisian, who had tried to immigrate to Germany, drove a stolen truck into a packed Berlin Christmas market. The death toll was 13, with 211 injured. Both attacks, and others not mentioned (for example, the London Bridge attacks on June 3, 2017), are consistent with immigrants posing a potential terrorist risk. By contrast, consider two recent terrorist attacks in the United States. On December 2, 2015, Rizwan Farook and Tashfeen Malik engaged in an armed terrorist attack in San Bernardino, California, that killed 14 and injured 22 people. Farook was American-born, while Malik, his wife, was a Pakistani immigrant.[22] On June 12, 2016, American-born Omar Mateen went on a shooting rampage at the Pulse, an Orlando nightclub. He killed 49 people and injured 53 others. There are many instances where a native-born citizen is radicalized and commits a terrorist act—for example, Major Nidal Malik Hasan, the Fort Hood shooter on November 5, 2009. Thus, casual empiricism, or the observation of a limited number of specific cases, can suggest either a link or no link between immigration and terrorist attacks, depending on the cases observed.

Actually, drawing a statistically inferred linkage based on a reasonably large unbiased sample of countries is a difficult challenge. In any given country, such as the United States, there may be millions of immigrants. Even when some of them commit terrorist attacks, the percentage of immigrants doing so is extremely small. Additionally, one must compare this percentage with that of native-born citizens who commit terrorist acts to ascertain whether immigrants pose the greater risk of terrorism. Both a greater stock of foreigners and a greater stock of native-born citizens can increase the likelihood of terrorist attacks. Thus, statistical inference is not so straightforward.

In a recent study, three researchers examine 20 Organization for Economic Co-operation and Development (OECD) countries that are hosts to immigrants and 187 countries of immigrant origin.[23] For 1980–2010, the study shows that the likelihood of a terrorist incident increases with the stock of foreigners, but this so-called scale effect *was not greater* than that associated with native-born citizens engaging in terrorist incidents. Simply put, a larger stock of native-born citizens augmented the terrorism risks as much or more than a larger stock of foreigners in the country! Thus, the study indicates that immigration does not necessarily impose a greater risk of terrorism than would arise with any increase in the native-born population. Moreover, these researchers do not find convincing evidence that Muslim immigrants impose a palpable risk of terrorism. This study also shows that any risk of immigrant-induced terrorism was assuaged by policies to assimilate foreigners and to protect their rights.

Does Democracy Facilitate or Inhibit Terrorism?

Most of my readers live in a democracy, thereby making this question and its answer of particular interest. The question is also germane from a policy perspective since there has been a clear American-led effort starting with the George W. Bush administration to push democracy on autocratic countries, leading to Western efforts to champion and support the Arab Spring, which consisted of a series of popular revolts and protests in North Africa and the Middle East. The Arab Spring started with the Tunisian Revolution on December 17, 2010, and then spread to Libya, Egypt, Syria, Iraq, and elsewhere. Arab Spring–related protests also took place in Bahrain, Iran, Jordan, Lebanon, Morocco, Omar, and elsewhere. Notably, civil war ensued in Libya, Syria, and Yemen following the Arab Spring. Have the regime changes induced by the Arab Spring been less conducive to terrorism as autocratic regimes were replaced? Unfortunately, the answer is no in the short and medium run, since Arab Spring–induced political violence (civil wars, coups, and protests) is often associated with terrorism. As indicated later, nascent and partial democracies are prone to terrorism, as a weak or emerging government lacks the apparatus to protect lives and property.

Democracy possesses characteristics that can both promote and inhibit terrorism. So-called *strategic factors* may promote terrorism by facilitating terrorists' operations and protecting their safety.[24] These factors include freedom of association, freedom of movement, rights to privacy, restraints on executive powers, and rights to due process. Some democracies protect the rights to bear arms, which may further facilitate terrorist attacks. Another strategic factor is the freedom of the press, which allows for media coverage of terrorist attacks and terrorists' grievances. Press reporting can also spread the use of terrorist innovations to other groups, which is known as a demonstration or copycat effect. A graphic illustration of this effect occurred following the hijacking of Northwest

Airlines Flight 305 en route from Washington, DC, to Seattle on November 24, 1971. Hijacker D. B. Cooper (really an extortionist and not a terrorist) demanded $200,000 in twenty-dollar bills and four parachutes. These were given to him on the tarmac at the Seattle airport in exchange for the passengers and two of the attendants. He then demanded to be flown to Mexico via Reno, Nevada. While en route to Reno, Cooper parachuted from the rear door of the Boeing 727 at ten thousand feet and was never seen again. One of the two training parachutes used during his jump had had its panels sewn shut so that it would not open. At the time of his daring jump, the wind-chill was 69 below zero outside of the plane and Cooper was clad in a blue business suit, so that his likelihood of survival was virtually nil. Nevertheless, his innovative method was then copied unsuccessfully by seventeen other hijackers, necessitating that airline manufacturers redesign the Boeing 727, DC-8, and DC-9, so that their rear doors could not be opened during flight.[25]

There are two essential characteristics of democracies that inhibit terrorism. The first inhibitor comes from *political access* or *political participation* that allows citizens to express their preferences through voting. Any held grievance can give rise to a vote for change. People can coalesce into political action groups, lobbies, or parties to push an agenda through elections.[26] A second democratic inhibitor of terrorism rests with liberal democracies' mandate to protect lives and property. Leaders in democracies that fail this mandate can be expected to be voted from office, as was true of President Jimmy Carter after his handling of the November 1979 takeover of the US Embassy in Tehran, Iran. This hostage situation lasted 444 days and included a disastrous attempt by the United States to rescue the hostages. Full democracies will deploy extreme measures following large terrorist attacks or a state of heightened threat to regain or maintain the confidence of the electorate that the government can ensure their safety. In such dire times, the electorate will tolerate the loss of some civil liberties. Following 9/11, the Bush administration set in motion the establishment of the Department of Homeland Security.[27] On October 7, 2001, his administration launched the US-led invasion of Afghanistan to remove the Taliban from power and to deal a devastating blow to al-Qaeda. The US Patriot Act also suspended certain liberties by, among other things, allowing for greater surveillance.

To judge the net effect of various forms of governments on terrorism, one must weigh the inhibitors and the promoters of terrorism associated with alternative governance systems or regimes. In the strictest autocracy, terrorists possess few strategic opportunities to engage in terrorism despite potential grievances that cannot be addressed through political participation. Such autocracies limit terrorism by greatly restricting freedoms. Any terrorist acts are dealt with in a harsh manner regardless of collateral consequences. This is aptly illustrated by the Russian response to the Chechen terrorists' takeover of the Moscow Theater, which resulted in the capture of eight hundred hostages on October 23, 2002. After the terrorists murdered some hostages and negotiations stalled, Russian Special Forces stormed the theater on October 26, 2002. Prior to the raid, the Russian forces pumped an incapacitating gas into the ventilation system, killing over a hundred hostages and seriously sickening many others. At the conclusion of the raid, some forty-two Chechen rebels lay dead.[28]

Next consider a full democratic regime wherein the two dominating forces that curb terrorism are the relative lack of grievances, owing to the fullest possible political access, and the protection of lives and property, owing to liberal democratic ideals. Adherence to these ideals serves to offset countervailing strategic factors when the risks of terrorism are elevated. Thus, full democracies generally display little terrorism, except for some imported attacks.

Finally consider *anocracies*, which are regimes that fall somewhere between autocracies and democracies in their level of democratic freedoms. Examples include Chile, Mexico, and

Pakistan. In anocracies, would-be terrorists possess greater strategic avenues than in autocracies or democracies to participate in terrorist incidents. By limiting political access, compared to full democracies, anocracies offer their citizens reduced means to air their grievances. Without such means, these grievances may result in terrorism. Because anocracies possess less inherent commitment and capacity than democracies to protect lives and property, more terrorist attacks are also likely.

Imagine regime types arranged from strict autocracy at the far left and full democracy at the far right along a linear scale with anocracy in the middle. Further imagine that this scale is the horizontal axis of a two-dimensional diagram, with the number of terrorist incidents associated with each regime type measured on the vertical axis. Given the discussion above, the resulting plot of terrorist incidents is a hill-shaped graph with the greatest number of incidents at some middle regime values corresponding to anocracies. A recent empirical analysis of regime types and terrorism finds precisely this hill-shaped relationship for a global sample of countries during 1970–2012, controlling for other terrorism influences.[29] This hill-shaped relationship held for domestic *or* transnational terrorism. Furthermore, it characterized not only the venue country, but also the perpetrators' origin country.

This finding can be related back to the Arab Spring and, I believe, the ill-advised effort to transform autocracies into democracies as a means of reducing terrorism. This policy changes autocracies into transient and partial democracies, which are anocracies. Empirical evidence shows that, as such, these governments are associated with all types of political violence, including terrorism and civil war. For the latter, consider Libya and Syria as stark instances of intrastate civil wars. If such autocracy busting is pursued, then adequate checks must be instituted to address the likely increase in terrorism and other forms of political violence.

What Is the Role of Failed States in Terrorism?

Failed states cannot exercise control over their entire territory and lack the ability to govern. These countries' rule of law and governing institutions are weak. In 2017, examples of failed states include Afghanistan, Iraq, Libya, Pakistan, Somalia, South Sudan, Syria, and Yemen. Terrorist groups tend to cluster in these failed states, resulting in domestic terrorism that the host country possesses little ability to address. Moreover, terrorist groups in such states can send their operatives to other countries to launch transnational terrorist attacks. A recent instance is the Manchester Arena suicide bombing on May 22, 2017, by Salman Abedi, who had recently returned from a visit to Libya and Syria. In Iraq, Syria, and Yemen, indigenous terrorist groups have used the Internet to radicalize sympathizers to perform terrorist attacks abroad. For Libya and Syria, the downside of the Arab Spring again surfaces.

What Is the Role of the Media in Promoting Terrorism?

Clearly, modern advances in satellite communications gave terrorists a world stage, aptly illustrated by the 1972 Munich Olympics abduction and murder of nine Israeli athletes. Another instructive example of media's unintended promotion of transnational terrorism concerns the skyjacking of TWA Flight 847 en route from Athens to Rome on June 14, 1985. This Boeing 727-200 aircraft was carrying 136 Americans, 2 Italians, 6 Greeks, 1 West German, 3 Australians, 1 Sudanese, 1 Ethiopian, 1 Egyptian, and 2 Lebanese. Ten minutes after takeoff, the two Lebanese hijackers stormed the cockpit and ordered pilot John L. Testrake to fly to Beirut. He complied and set a heading for Beirut. When in the vicinity of the Beirut airport, Testrake requested and was denied permission to land on the runway, which had been blocked by firetrucks and other service vehicles. After circling until the plane was critically low on fuel, Testrake issued a frantic plea: "He has pulled a hand-grenade pin and is ready to blow up the aircraft if he has to. We must land at Beirut. No alternative." The blockading vehicles were then removed from the runway and the plane landed without mishap.[30]

Over the next four days, the hijacked plane made two landings in Algiers and two further landings in Beirut. To heighten the drama, the hijackers murdered Robert Dean Stetham, a twenty-three-year-old navy steelworker and diver, and threw his body onto the tarmac during the second stopover in Beirut on June 15. The world witnessed this cowardly act, meant to show the hijackers' resolve. During the plane's second stopover in Algiers, the hijackers made the following demands: (1) the release of all Arab prisoners from Israeli jails, (2) the withdrawal of Israeli forces from Lebanon, (3) the withdrawal of the Southern Lebanese Army from Lebanon, and (4) the transport of Ali Atwah from Athens to Algiers. Atwah was part of the three-man hijacking squad, but failed to secure a seat on Flight 847 because it had been sold out. His suspicious behavior led to his arrest after the flight departed without him. Truth is sometimes stranger than fiction! On June 15, Atwah was flown to Algiers and reunited with the other two hijackers in exchange for the Greek passengers. Throughout the hijacking, hostages were sequentially released in return for refueling, release of some prisoners held in Israel, and other creature comforts.

On June 17, the plane landed for the third time in Beirut and did not take off again because pilot Testrake had convincingly faked engine failure. The Shiite Amal militia, headed by Nabih Berri, reinforced the hijackers. The remaining forty or so hostages were removed from the plane and spread out among different hideouts throughout Beirut to head off a potential rescue mission, given the presence of a US aircraft carrier near Lebanon. Just the three-man crew remained on the hijacked plane until the incident finally ended on June 30. Until its conclusion, the incident dominated the news worldwide. At one point on June 19, three ABC news correspondents were permitted to interview pilot Testrake as he leaned out of the cockpit window to converse with the reporters on the tarmac.

The hijacking of TWA Flight 847 became a media circus that encouraged many future hijackings in the 1980s. At the hijacking's conclusion, the hijackers secured the release of over seven hundred Arab prisoners from Israeli jails. Berri extracted a promise from President Reagan that the United States would not launch any retaliatory raid against Lebanon. On June 30, the terrorists held a press conference to air their views before going free.

Although the media are not the cause of terrorism, their reporting gives the terrorists the publicity that they crave to advertise their cause, attract recruits, and terrorize the public. Today the Internet serves these same needs of the terrorists.

Prime Minister Margaret Thatcher often called for a blackout of all news reporting of terrorist incidents. Unfortunately, such a blackout plays into hands of terrorists by taking away a cherished civil liberty. Following the London Bridge and Borough Market terrorist attacks on June 3, 2017, CNN reported that Prime Minister Theresa May called for closer regulations of the Internet as a counterterrorism device. Not only do such regulations limit civil liberties, but they are also impractical and ineffective given encryption apps.

We must remember that the media also help in the fight against terrorism by alerting the public to threats and ongoing attacks. The Internet offers a means for citizens to alert the authorities of suspicious behavior. In some instances, the media may result in arrests—for example, the newspaper publication of the Unabomber's manifesto resulted in Theodore Kaczynski being turned in by his brother in April 1996. Moreover, the media can expose the hypocrisy of the terrorists, thus reducing their support. Finally, the media provide accounts of terrorist incidents that are compiled by researchers into event data sets for research purposes.[31]

3

ROLE OF TERRORIST GROUPS

What Is a Terrorist Group?

The main "player" or participant in terrorist attacks is the *terrorist group*; hence, it is essential that such a group be defined. A terrorist group is a subnational collective of individuals who pursue a common political goal through the practice of terrorist acts.[1] As mentioned in chapter 1, terrorist acts consist of violent attacks, or the threat of such attacks, intended to influence an audience beyond the immediate noncombatant victims. In a democracy, this audience is the voting constituency, who can pressure elected officials into granting some of the terrorist group's political demands. When the Abu Nidal Organization (ANO) staged its daring simultaneous armed assaults at Schwechat and Fiumicino Airports in Vienna and Rome, respectively, on the morning of December 27, 1985, the message was political, the tactic was a brutal attack, and the audience was the world community.[2] The unfortunate casualties at the two airports served to communicate with this community. At the Vienna airport, three people were killed and thirty-seven wounded; at the Rome airport, thirteen people were killed and seventy-three wounded. Pictures of the horrible carnage at the nearby coffee bar at the Rome airport made the cover page of magazines and newspapers worldwide. Both attacks took place at the check-in counter for Israeli El Al airline, leaving no doubt that the attacks supported an independent Palestinian state. At both attack venues, the terrorists used Kalashnikov assault weapons and grenades, resulting in two scenes of utter bedlam as the terrorists and security guards engaged in a pitched battle that placed hundreds of travelers in the crossfire. The Vienna attack commenced at 9:00 a.m., and the Rome attack commenced at 9:15 a.m. These assaults marked the first complex simultaneous terrorist attacks at distinct locations by a terrorist organization. Such simultaneous attacks were later copied by al-Qaeda (Afghanistan), Lashkar-e-Taiba (Pakistan), Islamic State in Iraq and Syria (ISIS), and other terrorist groups as a means of ratcheting up audience anxiety and pressure on elected officials.

Like terrorism, the definition of terrorist groups is not always agreed upon by researchers and policymakers. A major point of contention includes the *inclusiveness* of the definition of terrorist groups.[3] An inclusive definition concerns any subnational group that applies terrorist tactics to promote its political agenda. More exclusive definitions require that the group primarily or exclusively use terrorism as opposed to some combination of tactics that allows for terrorism, legitimate political protest, or guerrilla attacks against the military. Most terrorist groups resort to both terrorist and legitimate means to get their message across. For example, many terrorist groups have a political wing to pursue their political agenda. These groups include the Palestine Liberation Organization (PLO), the Irish Republican Army (IRA), and Euskadi Ta Askatasuna (ETA) (the Basque separatist terrorists in Spain). Many groups may also use urban guerrilla tactics to attack the police, the National Guard, or the military, as was true of the IRA, ETA, the Front de Libération Nationale (FLN) (Algeria), Irgun Zvai Leumi (Zionist), and the Stern Gang (Zionist). Thus, basing the definition of terrorist group on its primarily or exclusively relying on terrorism would eliminate many important groups from consideration and, I believe, would serve no useful purpose. In fact, terrorist groups' choice of tactics is an important topic of analysis with essential policy questions—for example, does outlawing nonviolent protest cause more terrorism?

In other instances, exclusion may be based on whether or not the group holds territory, such as al-Qaeda in the Islamic Maghreb (AQIM), al-Qaeda in the Arabian Peninsula (AQAP), Fuerzas Armadas Revolucionaire de Colombia (FARC), and ISIS. Such groups control territory from which to launch attacks, extort the local population, hold kidnap victims, exploit natural resources, or seek safe haven. Terrorist groups in weak or failing states control territory and represent some of the world's most important terrorist organizations. Once again, the exclusion of such territory-controlling groups would, I contend, unnecessarily eliminate many key terrorist groups from consideration. Thus, I strongly abide by the inclusive definition.

Terrorist groups can range greatly in size.[4] The largest terrorist groups have over ten thousand members, such as FARC, Farabundo Martí National Liberation Front (now a political party in El Salvador), ISIS, New People's Army (in the Philippines), Moro National Liberation Front (now a political party in the Philippines), and the PLO, whereas the smallest terrorist groups have fewer than one hundred members, such as Animal Liberation Front (International), Combatant Communist Cells (Belgium), Tupac Amaru Revolutionary Army (Peru), and Japanese Red Army. Intermediate-size terrorist groups contain over one hundred but less than a thousand members, as is true of Abu Sayyaf (the Philippines), Democratic Front for the Liberation of Palestine (DFLP), and Jemaah Islamiyah (Indonesia). Still other terrorist groups contain over one thousand members but less than ten thousand members, such as ETA, Lashkar-e-Taiba, National Liberation Army of Colombia, and Shining Path (Peru). Larger terrorist groups tend to survive longer and may engage in both terrorism and guerrilla warfare. Some groups of one thousand or more members control territory. Lone wolf terrorists may be inspired by terrorist organizations to commit an attack on behalf of the group. Anis Amri, a Tunisian, was a lone wolf terrorist who plowed a stolen truck into pedestrians at a Christmas market in Berlin on December 19, 2016.[5] In recent years, there are many instances of lone wolf terrorist incidents that are difficult to protect against because the perpetrator may not be known to the authorities.

About 75 percent of terrorist groups have a single base country of operations, while about 20 percent of groups operate from two countries.[6] Tactically, terrorist groups engage in both domestic and transnational terrorist attacks. The latter kind of attack is riskier but garners more global attention. Most terrorist groups diversify their portfolio of attacks in order to be less predictable to the authorities charged with counterterrorism activities. Even though most groups use bombings as their primary mode of attack, they also execute armed attacks, assassinations, kidnappings, and other types of attacks to throw off the authorities. This mixing of tactics is analogous to a pitcher who excels with his fast ball, throwing curves and sliders on occasions to keep the batter off balance. Mixing one's plays or attacks is an optimal game-theoretic strategy.

What Are the Alternative Types of Terrorist Groups?

A main distinguishing feature of terrorist groups is their ideology, which is linked to the groups' primary political goal. Generally, terrorist groups are associated with one of four basic ideologies: right wing, nationalist/separatist, left wing, and religious fundamentalist. Right-wing terrorist groups may desire a return to the status quo. In specific instances, these groups protest immigration, racial equality, abortion, government actions, or some social change. The Ku Klux Klan (KKK), the Militia of Montana (MOM), and the Mozambican National Resistance Movement (RENAMO) are examples of right-wing terrorist groups. For example, RENAMO is an anti-communist militant group, initially sponsored in 1975 by the Rhodesian

Central Intelligence Organization, to oppose the then ruling government of Mozambique. Nationalist/separatist terrorist groups seek an autonomous state within an existing country. The desired autonomous country may include the whole or a portion of the current country. Well-known nationalist/separatist terrorist groups include ETA, IRA, Kurdistan Workers' Party (Iraq), PLO, and the Popular Front for the Liberation of Palestine (PFLP). Left-wing or leftist terrorist groups are generally anticapitalist or Marxist in orientation and include Animal Liberation Front, Farabundo Martí National Liberation Front, FARC, First of October Anti-Fascist Resistance Group (GRAPO) (Spain), Japanese Red Army, and Shining Path. A fourth ideological basis for terrorist groups is religious fundamentalism; such groups grew in dominance during and after the 1990s. Although these religious fundamentalist terrorist organizations can represent all of the great religions (for example, Kach was a Jewish fundamentalist terrorist group), Islamic extremist terrorist groups are disproportionately represented among such groups.[7] Notable religious fundamentalist terrorist groups include al-Qaeda, al-Shabaab (Somalia), Armed Islamic Group (Algeria), Boko Haram (Nigeria), Hamas (Gaza), Hezbollah (Lebanon), ISIS, Jemaah Islamiyah, and Taliban (Afghanistan and Pakistan). These groups often protest Western influences and policies in their homeland. In some instances, religious fundamentalist groups pursue regionwide regime change—for example, Jemaah Islamiyah desires a panregional Islamic state in Southwest Asia. ISIS wants to establish a caliphate in Iraq and Syria; Hamas wants to establish an independent Palestinian state. In an effort to purge US influence from the Arabian Peninsula, al-Qaeda called for a holy war (fatwa) against the United States.

These religious fundamentalist terrorist groups are out for maximum casualties; thus they do not provide warnings prior to specific attacks. As described in chapter 1, the increasing carnage of terrorism since the rising dominance of these groups is reflected by the greater proportion of terrorist attacks with casualties (deaths or injuries) after the mid-1990s. Many religious fundamentalist groups view all nonbelievers as legitimate targets, so that attacks can be aimed at women and children. Their tactics may include suicide bombings. Moreover, these groups may resort to chemical, biological, radiological, or nuclear terrorist attacks (see chapter 7).[8]

In a sample of 586 terrorist groups covering 1970–2007, 37 percent were left wing, 37 percent were nationalist/separatist, 21 percent were religious fundamentalist, and 5 percent were right wing. However, these percentages changed over time with nationalist/separatist and religious fundamentalist groups coming to represent the two largest proportions of active groups in the 2000s. Almost 70 percent of religious fundamentalist terrorist groups began their operations after 1990.[9] The geographical distribution of terrorist groups also altered over time as right-wing groups declined in numbers and religious fundamentalist groups increased in numbers. Left-wing groups are concentrated in Europe and Central Asia, Latin America, and North America, while religious fundamentalist groups are concentrated in the Middle East and North Africa, sub-Saharan Africa, and South Asia. Nationalist/separatist terrorist groups are distributed throughout the world, with lots of recent activity in the Middle East and North Africa, sub-Saharan Africa, and East Asia and Pacific. The changing geographic distribution of terrorist groups over time is partly responsible for the changing geographic distribution of terrorist attacks before and after 9/11 that is shown in chapter 4. Leftist groups are more associated with middle- and high-income democracies, while religious fundamentalist groups are more associated with low- and middle-income autocracies and partly free democracies.[10]

How Do Terrorist Groups Attract and Retain Members?

The different types of terrorist groups rely on diverse methods to attract their members. Left-wing, nationalist/separatist, and right-wing terrorist groups recruit members with strongly held political views, consistent with those of the group. Those views have to be sufficiently held that recruits would be willing to assume the considerable risk associated with engaging in attacks. Moreover, recruits must realize that leaving the group may be difficult or impossible.[11]

Religious fundamentalist terrorist groups employ different tactics than other ideologies to recruit their members. These groups often rely on kinship, long-term friendships, and worship for identifying committed potential members.[12] Such tight ties also curb greatly authorities' ability to infiltrate these groups, while fostering a sense of camaraderie. Through places of worship, the group looks for potential recruits who are well known to other members and who are recently alienated from society. Camaraderie works particularly well in gaining the commitment of these alienated individuals, as they now find a place for themselves. Their alienation and newly found meaning in the terrorist group often allow them to engage in a suicide attack.[13]

Some ultraorthodox religious groups may limit their children's opportunities by providing religious-based education that offers a poor skill set for future employment. Grown individuals may come to possess little or no economic opportunities outside of providing services to the religious group, thus making them amenable to participating in extremist activities, including suicide missions. These children are raised in a sterile environment with little or no outside contact, so that their entire world is inwardly drawn and they are loyal to the elders and other group members. This imposed isolation may strike many readers as extremely cynical, but those who argue that extremists limit their children's opportunities indicate convincing supporting evidence.[14]

For all terrorist groups, backlash, or a negative reaction to stringent government counterterrorism measures, may also serve as a recruitment mechanism. A common terrorist tactic is to push the government to overreact to a brutal terrorist attack as a means of attracting members. Overly harsh government reactions, such as torture or summary executions, can alienate the general public, thereby gaining recruits for the terrorist group. Governments can be overzealous in limiting civil liberties, thereby losing support among their constituency, which may come to view the government as worse than the terrorists.[15] Recruitment to the terrorist group may also follow large-scale successful terrorist missions. This has been used by ISIS to attract alienated Western and Central Asian youths. Today's terrorist groups have mastered the Internet as a means for recruiting members to a calling that is cast as an exciting life with strong friendships. The Internet also provides a means for attracting lone wolf terrorists.

What Is the Role of Service Provision by Terrorist Groups?

In recent years, religious fundamentalist groups (for example, Hamas, Hezbollah, Lashkar-e-Taiba, and Taliban) offer members and their families a wide range of social services (for example, healthcare, soup kitchens, and education) in order to gain members' loyalty and commitment. When, for instance, the Lebanese government did a poor job in supplying these services, Hezbollah stepped in and provided them, thereby becoming the de facto government. The provision of social services allowed Hamas to win the governance of Gaza. At times, these social services can be used for a sinister purpose— namely, to induce suicide attacks. The terrorist group can withhold services from noncooperative members and their families, thereby exercising significant leverage over members. A designated suicide terrorist may have little choice but to sacrifice himself if it means that his family will be provided with the necessary social services. Family ties are strong in this part of the world. Empirical evidence shows that service-providing religious fundamentalist groups have engaged in more suicide terrorist incidents than other terrorist groups.[16]

To counter the recruitment draw of service provision, the government must be put on a proper footing to be able to

supply these services, thereby taking away the monopoly provision of the terrorist group. This may require outside funding
by foreign governments with an interest in the stability of the
state. Once outside funding is involved, corruption becomes
a consideration because the funding may not be used as intended as officials siphon off the money for their purposes.

Why Do Some Terrorist Groups Resort to Suicide Terrorism, While Others Do Not?

Prior to the October 23, 1983, suicide bombing on the US Marines
barracks in Beirut during a US-led multinational peacekeeping
operation, there had been only a few suicide terrorist attacks.
Incidents of suicide attacks really expanded in numbers after
1995.[17] During 1968–1990, the dominant left-wing and nation-
alist/separatist terrorist groups did not believe in sacrificing
themselves for the cause during operations. Apparently, they
believed that living to fight another day did more to bolster
the cause. Additionally, these terrorists did not want to kill indiscriminately since they wanted to win over a constituency
to lobby the government for their political agenda. Often such
terrorists issued advance warnings of their attacks to limit the
carnage. This is ironically illustrated by the horrific Omagh car
bombing by the Real IRA (RIRA) on August 15, 1998, which
killed 29, including women and children, and injured 220
people. The RIRA was a splintered group of the Provisional
IRA (PIRA), which was in peace talks with the British government at the time. Unintentionally, RIRA's advance warning
prior to the Omagh explosion herded people to the vicinity of
the car bomb, thereby maximizing the casualties. The attack
led to strong condemnation by the public and the PIRA, and
resulted in an eventual apology by the RIRA. Public reaction
was so negative that the RIRA agreed to disarm.[18]

After the 1990s, many religious fundamentalist terrorist
groups adopted suicide attacks as a tactic, for a number
of reasons. First, these attacks placed greater pressures on

democratic governments to concede to terrorists' demands. One influential study indicates that some suicide campaigns induced moderate concessions from democratic governments (for example, the US peacekeeping troop withdrawal from Beirut in February 1984 following the barracks bombing, and the Israeli partial withdrawal from Lebanon in 1985).[19] Second, suicide terrorist attacks kill and injure far more people than most conventional attacks, thereby capturing more media coverage. Suicide attacks kill around eleven to twelve people on average, while conventional attacks kill around two. Third, this greater death toll generates more societal anxiety, a goal of the terrorists. Fourth, suicide terrorist attacks are harder to guard against since deaths can result even if the bomb is detonated outside of the intended venue, as illustrated by the Manchester Arena incident on May 22, 2017. Fifth, large-scale suicide attacks can penetrate "hard targets"—military compounds or airport security checkpoints. A recent tactic is to explode a suicide bomb at a checkpoint or front gate, thereby leaving an opening for a second wave of armed terrorists to enter unimpeded. Sixth, suicide bombers can position themselves beside the largest number of people in order to wreak a greater casualty toll. Essentially, a suicide bomber is like a precision-guided munition, but smarter. Seventh, suicide attacks are low cost if the bomber's life is ignored, making such attacks available to groups with limited means. These attacks are also low-tech operations.

Let's return to the hard-target rationale for suicide bombings. Religious fundamentalist groups deployed suicide bombers to hit fortified targets as a means to gain entry. As mentioned earlier, a first wave of suicide terrorists can work in tandem with a subsequent wave of armed terrorists to enter fortified military compounds, embassies, or prisons. The provision of social services can motivate some members to carry out these complex attacks despite the ultimate personal cost. Terrorist groups assign older and more educated individuals to execute suicide attacks on the highest-valued, and often most-secured, targets.[20] Apparently, these groups have an inexhaustible supply of volunteer suicide terrorists, so that the groups are rational to deploy the most capable operative to such missions.

What Are the Major Sources of Support for Terrorist Groups?

Small terrorist groups require modest funding since most terrorist attacks are inexpensive. Many leftist groups during the 1970s and 1980s funded their operations through bank robberies (for example, the Red Army Faction in Germany or the Italian Red Brigades). Other groups extorted money from the families of kidnapped victims. Still other groups relied on their members or supporters for funding.

Larger terrorist groups drew from a host of funding sources. For example, the IRA gained revenue from gaming machines in pubs and from money sent from abroad. Apparently, Irish Americans were a huge source of financial support for the IRA. It is well known that the Tamil diaspora in Western Europe, North America, Australia, and India sent funds to support the Tamil Tigers' fight for independence against the Sri Lankan government. This was true even though the Tamil Tigers deployed many suicide terrorist attacks against Sri Lankan targets that resulted in large, indiscriminate casualty tolls.

Greater funds are needed for groups that provide training facilities for their members and those of other groups, as was true of the PLO and al-Qaeda. Often these groups charge trainees for their training in order to defray the cost of the required infrastructure. Osama bin Laden initially used some of his personal funds to establish and finance al-Qaeda in Afghanistan. ISIS, and other groups that controlled territory, extorted money from people under their control. ISIS also acquired funds from stolen antiquities, captured oil facilities, and kidnapping ransoms. At times, charities underwrote some terrorist groups, often through money collected from remittances or donations from the country's diaspora. In other instances, the group engaged in legitimate commercial ventures. Illegitimate activities, such as counterfeiting luxury goods or money, supported some groups' terrorist attacks. Illegal drugs also funded some terrorist activities—the cocaine trade once helped support FARC in Colombia. Quite simply, terrorist groups rely on many means of financial support. When the authorities sever one means of support, these groups locate alternative means.[21]

What Are the Role and Implications of State Sponsorship of Terrorist Groups?

The definition of terrorism presented in chapter 1 rules out state terror but allows for state sponsorship, in which a country assists the terrorist group. This aid includes supplying weapons, gathering intelligence, giving training, supplying funding, providing security, or providing safe passage. For some nascent terrorist groups, state sponsorship may be an essential source of initial financing. The most critical form of state sponsorship is the state's provision of a safe haven in which the group can train and seek sanctuary when it is not engaging in attacks. A classic instance of safe haven was provided to Osama bin Laden's al-Qaeda by the Taliban in the tribal areas of Afghanistan during al-Qaeda's rise to prominence prior to 9/11.[22] This sponsorship and the Taliban's failure to turn in bin Laden to the United States after 9/11 resulted in the US-led invasion of Afghanistan during October 2001. The subsequent Afghanistan War continues to this day!

There was a lot of state sponsorship of terrorism during the last decade of the Cold War, with groups such as the ANO, founded by Sabri al-Banna, serving as a terrorist group for hire. In fact, the ANO allegedly amassed $400 million in assets from its paid operations. During the 1980s, known as the decade of state sponsorship, Syria, Iraq, and Libya hired the services of the ANO and other groups. Countries use state sponsorship as a foreign policy tool to destabilize other governments and as an instrument of revenge in the hope that their support remains covert. State-sponsored terrorist attacks have frequently been more deadly than typical terrorist incidents, especially during the 1980s, when state-sponsored groups, such as the ANO, Hezbollah, or the PFLP, went for high body counts. Notable instances of state-sponsored attacks include the April 18, 1983, bombing of the US embassy in Beirut; the October 23, 1983, suicide car bombing of the US Marines barracks in Beirut; the October 23, 1983, suicide car bombing of the French paratroopers headquarters in Beirut; the December 21, 1988, downing of Pan Am Flight 103 over Scotland; and the September 19, 1989, downing of Union des Transport (UTA) Flight 772 over Chad. All of these state-sponsored incidents involved mass casualties. The three Beirut attacks were executed by Islamic Jihad (really Hezbollah) under the backing of Iran, whereas the downings of the Pan Am and UTA flights were executed by Libyan intelligence agents.[23] State-sponsored terrorism continued after the end of the Cold War but at a somewhat smaller level.

Recent research shows that state sponsorship, especially in terms of safe havens, offers pluses and minuses to resident terrorist groups. The obvious plus is sanctuary and the ability to establish an infrastructure with training facilities. Without the fear of a host-country attack, the terrorists have more resources from which to launch attacks abroad against other countries' interests. The subtle minus may come following a large transnational terrorist attack that the targeted country traces back to the perpetrating terrorist group in its sanctuary state. The targeted country will then apply pressures on the sanctuary country, as the United States did to the Taliban after 9/11, to give up the perpetrators, provide helpful intelligence, or allow for some form of military retribution (for example, precision raids or drone strikes). The sanctuary country may comply to avoid a costly retaliatory attack or a full-scale foreign invasion, thereby affronting the host country's sovereignty. A host-country compliance can jeopardize the resident group's safety and survival. Research suggests that transnational terrorist groups face a greater survival risk when given safe haven compared to groups not given safe haven. Although safe haven may foster the group's internal stability, it may limit its long-term survival when the sanctuary country is challenged by a strong targeted country.[24]

How Do Terrorist Groups End?

One of the most important questions concerns how terrorist groups end their operations. By knowing groups' endings and their causes, policymakers can conceivably take actions to hasten the demise of terrorist groups.[25] Terrorist groups may end in ways that are both favorable and unfavorable to targeted governments. In this regard, the most favorable conclusion is the defeat of the terrorist group by government forces. On May 18, 2009, the Sri Lankan government forces soundly defeated the Tamil Tigers, thus ending a twenty-five-year terrorist campaign and civil war. The death toll from the civil war ranged between eighty thousand and one hundred thousand.

The capture or killing of a group's leader may not end a terrorist group, as aptly illustrated by the assassination of Osama bin Laden, the leader of al-Qaeda, by US Navy commandos on May 2, 2011. Other instances where the death of the group's leader did not end the group are Israel's assassinations of Ahmed Yassin on March 22, 2004, and Abdel Aziz al-Rantissi on April 17, 2004. Despite the murders of these Hamas leaders, the organization carried on as usual.

Smaller terrorist groups may end if key members are captured, which was true of the Combatant Communist Cells in Belgium, the Red Brigades in Italy, and 17 November in Greece. In these cases, captured terrorists provided the identity of most members to the authorities. In other instances, a terrorist group can end if it fails to maintain some popular support, as in the case of the Tupamaros in Uruguay during 1968–1972. Financed by kidnappings and bank robberies, the Tupamaros applied a brutal form of urban guerrilla warfare that failed to win over the working class, which these privileged students claimed to represent.[26] A terrorist group without a constituency must fear informants and an uphill fight to stay funded.

A terrorist group can end from splintering into two or more factions. Although the original group morphs with splintering, the authorities may now confront multiple threats, some more worrisome than others. The PLO splintered many times; derivative groups included Black September, PFLP, PFLP-General Command, and others. Often, but not always, the splintered group assumed a harder line than the original group. At times, splintering occurs if the government reached an accommodation with moderates in the group, thus leaving hardliners to form their own group. RIRA, responsible for the Omagh bombing in Northern Ireland in August 1998, is an example. From the government's viewpoint, a more favorable outcome arises when internal strife within the group results in disbandment and ceased attacks. The German RAF ended this way after issuing a final communication to the Reuters news agency on April 20, 1998. RAF started as the Baader-Meinhof Group in 1970 and transitioned into a second and third generation in the mid-1970s and 1980s, respectively. Each subsequent generation of this Marxist-Leninist group became more violent. With the collapse of communism and the public's growing disenchantment with socialism, the group saw little support for its views.

A much less favorable outcome from the viewpoint of the besieged government is when the terrorist group achieves victory by obtaining some or all of its demands. Irgun Zvai Leumi and Stern Gang achieved victory with the statehood of Israel. Similarly, the FLN gained victory with the independence of Algeria. There are numerous instances where nationalist/separatist groups obtained their political goals. A lesser form of victory for both the terrorists and the government is when the terrorists cease their operations and join the political process.

The latter was true of the IRA in Northern Ireland, Moro National Liberation Front in the Philippines, and Farabundo Martí National Liberation Front in El Salvador. One study of 648 terrorist groups during 1968–2006 finds that 23 percent of groups joined the political process or else achieved victory.[27] About a third of sample terrorist groups were still active in 2006.

What Are the Determinants of Terrorist Group Survival?

Some terrorist groups have survived for fifty or more years (for example, ETA, FARC, and PLO), while many groups ceased operations during their first year of operation. In the latter category, some terrorist groups were one-hit wonders that vanished after their initial terrorist attack. Based on a variety of data sources on terrorist groups, a recent study finds that 25 to 74 percent of terrorist groups did not survive beyond their first year of operations.[28] This is a larger survival percentage than the conventional wisdom that claims that 90 percent of terrorist groups do not last into a second year. Unlike this recent study, the conventional wisdom was not based on an empirical evaluation of the life span of terrorist groups. Data on terrorist groups were not available in the early 1990s, when the conventional wisdom emerged.[29] In the new study, the one-year failure percentage varies widely because different samples of terrorist groups are used that span diverse time periods. Also, the type of terrorist groups varies in the alternative samples. Some samples include just groups that engage in one or more transnational terrorist incidents, while other samples include all groups, even those that just do domestic terrorist attacks. Because left-wing terrorist groups have a higher first-year failure rate than nationalist/separatist, right-wing, and religious fundamentalist groups, group samples with more coverage of the pre-1990 period are likely to uncover a larger first-year failure rate, owing to the greater prevalence of more fragile left-wing groups.

With the accumulation of forty years of data on terrorist organizations' characteristics and operations, researchers can apply statistical methods to ascertain the determinants of these groups' survival. When groups end, these methods can be refined to identify what factors led to alternative endings. Groups' survival is likely to depend on groups' characteristics, their geographical location, their tactics, and base countries' characteristics.

In one recent study, the average duration of terrorist groups was about ten years, and around 68 percent of sample groups lasted for ten or fewer years. Larger terrorist groups operated longer. Compared to the other three ideologies, religious fundamentalist terrorist groups survived longer. Terrorist groups located in the Middle East and North Africa persisted longer than those in other regions of the world. None of this is good news for counterterrorism policy because religious fundamentalist groups are being created at a faster pace than those driven by other ideologies. Moreover, many religious fundamentalist terrorist groups are in the Middle East and North Africa and have large memberships. Examples include al-Nusra, AQAP, AQIM, al-Shabaab, Boko Haram, and ISIS. These findings underscore the need for targeted Western countries to pool efforts with countries in the region to annihilate these groups.

Terrorist groups with fewer casualties per attack survived somewhat longer than more carnage-prone groups, presumably because there was less public outcry to confront the group. Survival was more assured for those groups with multiple bases of operation, which allow such groups to transfer assets to where there is less host-country counterterrorism action. Generally, terrorist groups that diversified their attacks and executed fewer transnational terrorist attacks had a better survival prognosis. Thus, groups' tactics mattered for survival. Some base countries' characteristic bolstered group survival. By providing a more favorable environment for terrorist groups (see chapter 2), democracies generally added to the longevity of resident terrorist groups. Recall that democracies protect the rights of terrorists, allow for freedom of movement, permit freedom of association, and place greater restraints on the government. Competition among terrorist groups within the same country often augmented resident groups' life span, as governments' counterterrorism efforts were spread over more groups.[30] This is particularly worrisome for failed and failing states that often contain a number of terrorist groups.

What Are the Determinants of Alternative Ways That Terrorist Groups End?

Having identified some determinants of terrorist group survival, I next indicate some factors that influence alternative endings for these groups. I divide internal dissolution into two competing risks—splintering and joining the political process. The former reflects a within-group failure to pursue a common goal, while the latter suggests group unity to seek a goal through legitimate political means. I combine joining the political process with achieving victory insofar as both outcomes indicate that the terrorist groups have joined the established political order.[31]

For a sample of 586 terrorist groups during 1970–2007, 19 percent were defeated, 22 percent splintered, and 23 percent joined the political process or achieved victory. The remainder of the groups (36 percent) was still active at the end of the sample period. On average, active terrorist groups were larger in size than those that ended in defeat or splintered. These active terrorist groups also confronted stiffer competition in terms of the number of other groups in the same base country. In contrast, terrorist groups that ended by political participation or victory were the largest and faced fewer competitive terrorist groups in their base country. The largest shares of active terrorist groups were those of the nationalist/separatist and the religious fundamentalist groups. Left-wing groups succumbed more than other ideologies to defeat and, ironically, were also more apt to join the political process or achieve victory. No sample religious fundamentalist group achieved victory and only three joined the political process. In the sample, nationalist/separatist groups were the most susceptible to splintering, followed by left-wing groups.

When terrorist groups are scrutinized with appropriate statistical methods, there are some interesting, but sobering, findings. Religious fundamentalist terrorist groups are the least likely of the four ideologies to end by force or to join the political process. This is not good news for the authorities, who must confront a growing presence of such religious organizations. Not surprising, terrorist groups with broadly defined goals—empire, regime change, or social revolution—are less apt to join the political process or achieve concessions. This is also the case for groups seeking large-scale territorial change. Today's religious fundamentalist groups possess these broad goals. Moreover, terrorist groups with multiple bases are unlikely to end by force or splintering. This suggests that authorities must work with their counterparts in other countries to inhibit these multiple bases from becoming established. In recent years, this counterterrorism strategy has been unsuccessful, with ISIS establishing new bases in Afghanistan, Egypt, Libya, and Somalia. Obviously, such groups sought new bases in weak or failed states. Within each base country, terrorist group competition inhibits political solutions in ending each group. When confronted with multiple terrorist groups, a government-negotiated compromise with one group is generally unacceptable to another resident group, whose political aims differed markedly. Terrorist groups, based in the Middle East and North Africa are less apt to join the political process, compared to groups located elsewhere. The post-9/11 geographical shift of terrorist activities to religious fundamentalist terrorist groups in this region (see chapter 4) is not encouraging for curbing the longevity of terrorist groups. Group size has a negative impact on splintering, being defeated, or joining the political process, with the largest effect on limiting splintering.

These findings are helpful in guiding counterterrorism resources to where they may be most effective in eliminating terrorist groups. Such insights also aid in assessing the changing threat of terrorism.

How Do Terrorist Groups Organize Themselves?

Terrorist groups confront a trade-off between their capability and vulnerability. Tightly knit terrorist group structures brought down the Italian Red Brigades, the Baader-Meinhof Group (later known as the RAF), 17 November, Aum Shinrikyo (perpetrators of the sarin attack on the Tokyo subway on March 20, 1995), and other groups, as the capture of one or more members compromised the identity of large swaths of the group (see chapter 5 for more particulars). If, however, members are loosely linked so that one small cell of four or five members does not know the identity of other cells, then the group's vulnerability is greatly curtailed. However, this reduced vulnerability comes at the price of limiting mission complexity. With small independent cells, an operative unit is less capable of conducting involved missions such as 9/11 or the downing of Pan Am Flight 103.[32] From the public's perspective, there are both good and bad consequences when terrorists loosen their organizational structure.

One must always remember that terrorist groups learn from experience, which informs them on how to revamp their structure and their operations. For instance, each new generation of RAF terrorists discovered the group's weaknesses by studying past court case transcripts.[33] When RAF learned that the German police lifted members' fingerprints from the inside of refrigerators and from underneath toilet seats in RAF hideouts, members used a finger ointment to prevent future incriminating evidence. As successful innovations were developed by one terrorist group, other groups quickly copied them. Similarly, terrorist groups learned about past effective countermeasures of the authorities in order to limit their future effectiveness. Consider innovations that the authorities used to rescue the hostages of hijacked Lufthansa Flight 181, a Boeing 737. During the plane's unscheduled stopover in Mogadishu, Somalia, on October 17, 1977, the West German Grenzschutzgruppe Neun (GSG-9) commandos created a diversion at 2:00 a.m. with an ignited oil canister at the front of the cockpit. During the ensuing confusion, GSG-9 commandos gained entry through the plane's rear door and deployed stun grenades to incapacitate the hijackers.[34] This operation worked perfectly and redeemed somewhat the tarnished reputation of the German authorities after the botched operation at the 1972 Munich Olympics. Following the Mogadishu rescue, terrorists reacted violently to any perceived diversion during future skyjackings or barricade and other hostage-taking missions.

What Are Some of the Components of Terrorist Groups?

Large terrorist groups are generally composed of diverse components, charged with alternative tasks as a means to gain specialization of labor, thereby reducing the cost per mission. Terrorist groups' component parts plan attacks, recruit individuals, finance operations, seek constituency support, gather intelligence, train operatives, and spread propaganda. As mentioned earlier, a component of some large terrorist organizations provides for the social needs of a constituent population.

Frequently, these large terrorist groups possess a military wing for their operations and recruitment and a political wing for gaining local and international visibility. Examples include the ETA and Batasuna; the PLO and Fatah; the IRA and Sinn Féin; and Islamic Resistance and Hezbollah. These wings may work in concert or opposition. When wings work in tandem, counterterrorism against one wing may reduce the activities of both wings, contrary to the case wherein the wings work in opposition. The essential insight is that counterterrorism policy may have to be tailored to the relationship characterizing these wings.[35] Terrorist organizations are not always the unified whole that is typically presupposed.

Small terrorist organizations possess fewer components, thereby necessitating cells to perform multiple tasks—for example, recruiting, planning, and executing attacks. As a consequence, these cells engage in simple operations such as bombings. Without the benefits from the specialization of labor, small terrorist groups pose a modest threat and may be easily defeated, consistent with the earlier discussion.

Is There a Control Dilemma in Terrorist Groups?

Owing to terrorist organizations' diverse components, which may possess divergent agendas, the unity of these organizations is an ideal that is seldom borne out. Consider the group's leader and its financial manager. When terrorist organizations institute loose linkages among components for protection purposes, the financial manager likely knows information that is unknown to the leader regarding the assignment of funds to particular missions.[36] As a consequence, the leader must come to trust the actions of the manager, whose goals may not fully correspond to those of the leader. In fact, a less-committed manager may divert funds for his own enrichment, thus leaving less for the operation. This is a classic principal-agent control problem in which the leader (the principal) cannot observe the manager's (agent's) actions and must rely on the observed outcome of missions as a gauge of the manager's effort and commitment. Since missions may succeed because of chance (or good fortune) *or* adequate effort, the observed success is an imperfect signal on which to base the leader's evaluation of the manager. The associated principal-agent problem poses a dilemma: the group must exercise control on managers while remaining covert.[37]

In the absence of controls, terrorist funds may be diverted, wasted, or used inefficiently. These potential losses can be addressed by the leader through audits, incentive payments, and punishment, as done in business enterprises to address similar control issues when preferences do not align among the firms' different component participants. For terrorist organizations, such incentive-aligning actions could compromise the organization's secrecy. Audits and incentive payments leave a paper trail that can later identify group members. Punishments may push the disciplined agents to go to the authorities as a form of retribution.

A similar control problem applies to the leader and his field operatives, who carry out the attacks. Again, the leader must evaluate operatives' efforts based solely on the observed outcome of the attack. The second principal-agent problem results in a trade-off between operational security and tactical control. By exercising greater tactical control in the field, the leader must issue more commands that may be intercepted by the authorities, thereby compromising missions' secrecy and success. By giving the operatives less discretion in the field, the leader may reduce operatives' commitment as they sense reduced trust by the leader. Moreover, field operatives may observe information during the mission, not known to the leader, and must be free to respond optimally to such revelations. Thus, too much tactical control may limit missions' effectiveness.

If a trust problem develops between the leader and his manager or operatives, then the leader may withhold funds, thereby jeopardizing the mission's success. For example, the bombing of the World Trade Center on February 26, 1993, was done for less than $10,000, which is a very small amount given the intention to create a sufficient blast to topple both towers. Days after the attack, one of the cash-strapped terrorists, Mohammed A. Salameh, was apprehended when returning for his $400 deposit for the rented Ryder truck, which had held the bomb.[38] When asking for his deposit, Salameh explained that the Ford Econoline truck had been stolen and so he could not return it. His arrest as he walked away from the Ryder rental office, deposit in hand, eventually led to the capture of the rest of the cell.

There are a number of implications that this trust-and-control dilemma has for the practice of counterterrorism. Most notable is the realization that fewer resources may be needed for counterterrorism, given the implied inefficiency of many large-scale terrorist organizations. As terrorist attacks fail, the authorities should be especially vigilant, as the leader may exercise greater future tactical control through enhanced communications. The authorities need to use the Internet and the media to sow the seeds of distrust between terrorist leaders and their agents. Also, the authorities must search for accounting records, especially in large-scale terrorist organizations.

4

EFFECTIVENESS
OF COUNTERTERRORISM

What Are the Primary Tools of Counterterrorism?

Counterterrorism consists of actions by a government to inhibit terrorist attacks, to lessen their consequences, and to speed postattack recovery. Effective countermeasures can inhibit terrorist attacks by curtailing an attack's likelihood of success or anticipated payoff to the perpetrators. Generally, counterterrorism is divided into two broad categories: proactive and defensive measures.

Proactive policies are offensive because a government confronts the terrorists or their supporters directly. These actions may limit terrorists' resources, finances, safe havens, infrastructure, or sponsorship. In terms of sponsorship, the US-led invasion of Afghanistan on October 7, 2001, was aimed at the ruling Taliban government, which had provided sanctuary and support to Osama bin Laden and al-Qaeda, the perpetrators of the 9/11 skyjackings. Since 9/11, the United States has used drone attacks against al-Qaeda-affiliated groups in Afghanistan, Pakistan, Somalia, Yemen, and elsewhere to kill members and to destroy terrorists' assets. Intelligence can be applied proactively to capture group members before a planned attack is carried out. If the authorities can infiltrate the terrorist group, then a tightly knit structure can be severely compromised. Unfortunately, such infiltration has become much more difficult as terrorist groups increasingly rely on family or childhood ties for recruiting members. Also, group structures are now more loosely linked so that the compromise of one or a few members results in few arrests (see chapters 3 and 5).[1]

Proactive measures assume myriad other forms. After 9/11, there was an international effort to limit terrorist funding. For instance, bank deposits over a set limit required the depositor to fill out paperwork, known as a suspicious activity report (SAR). Charities with alleged terrorist ties were identified and shut down as a means to curb contributions that were being channeled to support terrorism. Even before 9/11, the International Monetary Fund (IMF) and the World Bank tried to coordinate efforts to reduce money laundering that funded terrorism and drug trafficking.[2] These efforts were enhanced in the wake of 9/11. Retaliatory raids as a punitive action following a terrorist act is another proactive measure. On November 16, 2015, France launched massive airstrikes against the stronghold of the Islamic State in Iraq and Syria (ISIS) in Raqqa, Syria, in retribution for the group's coordinated attacks in Paris on November 13, 2015, that killed 130. Another proactive measure involves the assassination of a terrorist group's leader, such as the US Navy SEALs operation on May 2, 2011, in Abbottabad, Pakistan, that killed Osama bin Laden. The Israeli government used targeted killings of terrorist leaders and operatives over the last decades as a means to disrupt a group's operation. Prime instances include the assassinations of Ahmed Yassin on March 22, 2004, and Abdel Aziz Rantisi on April 17, 2004. Yassin and Rantisi were the cofounders of Hamas; Rantisi had taken over the leadership of Hamas following the assassination of Yassin. Apache helicopters fired missiles to kill both men in Gaza City.[3]

Defensive actions, the other main kind of counterterrorism, protect potential targets either by making attacks more costly for terrorists or by reducing their chances of success. After an attack, effective defensive measures can limit the losses.

Consider the erection of cement barriers on the perimeters of federal buildings. By blocking a potential car bomb from the immediate vicinity of the building, a successful attack should kill fewer people and limit property damages. On April 19, 1995, Timothy McVeigh, a member of the right-wing Michigan Militia, parked a bomb-laden 1993 Ford truck in front of the Alfred P. Murrah Federal Building in Oklahoma City. The approximately five-hundred-pound bomb killed 169 and injured more than 500 people. The huge blast caused the front facade of the building to collapse.[4]

Many defensive responses are reactive because they are instituted only after past incidents have revealed vulnerabilities, which was true for the installation of cement barriers in front of some federal buildings following the Oklahoma City bombing. The installation of metal detectors in US airports on January 5, 1973, came only after a spate of skyjackings. There had been an average of twenty-seven US hijackings each year prior to 1973. The immediate effectiveness of metal detectors in drastically cutting the number of US skyjackings led to their installation in airports worldwide.[5] The use of bomb-detecting equipment to screen cargo luggage on commercial flights followed bombs downing Pan Am Flight 103 over Scotland on December 21, 1988, and UTA Flight 772 over Niger on September 19, 1989. The failed attempt by Robert Reid, the shoe bomber, to bring down American Airlines Flight 63 en route from Paris to Miami on December 22, 2001, has since required passengers in US airports to remove their shoes for screening.

Metal detectors and bomb-detecting devices are examples of technological barriers, which can be particularly effective when authorities continuously upgrade the technology in order to stymie attempts by terrorists to circumvent these barriers—for example, the use of plastic guns and non-nitrogen-based explosives. Obviously, screeners must be retrained periodically. When screeners are on duty, they must be vigilant and relieved on a regular basis.

Defensive measures often involve the hardening of targets. For example, in 1976 and again in 1985, the United States took actions to fortify its embassies. This now includes defensive perimeters around many US embassies. At important public events (for example, Times Square on New Year's Eve or the Boston Marathon), there is a major police presence. At Major League baseball games and other professional sporting events, patrons must pass through metal detectors. Targets are hardened everywhere one looks, but this poses an important dilemma because governments' resources are limited, so that not all potential targets can be hardened. High-valued targets that are easily defended and likely to be attacked must be hardened.[6] If two targets are equally valued (say, in terms of lives and property) and equally likely to be attacked, then the easier to defend should be hardened if there are insufficient resources to harden both.

Stiffening of penalties for terrorist offenses is another defensive measure intended to discourage would-be terrorists owing to the consequences of being caught either in the planning stage, during the attack, or after the attack. These harsher penalties are also meant to limit the willingness of others to assist terrorists in acquiring the weapons, planning the attack, or obtaining sanctuary. The effectiveness of these penalties as a deterrent hinges on three conditional probabilities: the likelihood of being caught, the likelihood of being convicted if caught, and the likelihood of serving a long sentence if convicted.[7] The intended deterrence fails if any one of these probabilities is small. If the likelihood of conviction is small *or* if the likelihood of receiving a stringent sentence is small, then being caught loses much of its deterrence value.

In the case of biological or chemical terrorist attacks, defensive measures involve the stockpiling of antibiotics for the former and the stockpiling of antidotes for the latter. Enhanced first-responder capabilities represent defensive responses that limit the deaths and damages following these and other kinds of terrorist attacks.

At the transnational level, the United Nations and other multilateral bodies (for example, the International Civil Aviation Organization) have passed conventions and treaties outlawing certain acts of terrorism—for instance, the downing of commercial aircrafts, the seizure of hostages, and the use of explosive bombs. One must remember that these well-intended conventions and treaties have no enforcement mechanism, relying instead on ratifying governments to carry out the conventions' mandate. I will return to their effectiveness at a later point in this chapter.

How Effective Are Proactive and Defensive Measures in Curbing Transnational Terrorism?

To address this question, I first consider proactive responses regarding transnational terrorist attacks, wherein two or more countries are targeted by the same terrorist groups. ISIS and al-Qaeda attacks against American, French, British, and other countries' interests fit this scenario. For proactive measures, there is a worrisome strategic interaction among targeted countries that limits their response. Given the common threat, proactive efforts by any targeted country to weaken the terrorist group provide benefits for all at-risk countries. Thus, if US drone attacks take out many of the leaders of al-Qaeda, then all would-be targeted countries are potentially safer. This results in a classic free-rider problem in which most targeted countries will do nothing, hoping that other countries will act to crush al-Qaeda. As a consequence, proactive measures are more likely to be underprovided. A proactive country is motivated by benefits that it confers on its own citizens, while ignoring the benefits derived by the citizens of other at-risk countries. This viewpoint reinforces the anticipated underprovision of proactive efforts.[8]

Given the proclivity to free ride, which country, if any, is apt to go after the common terrorist threat? The answer is simple: the country that is most negatively impacted will confront the terrorist group. In the 9/11 attack, the United States lost the most people and sustained the greatest property losses, followed by the United Kingdom. Understandably, the United States led the attack against the Taliban and al-Qaeda in October 2001, followed by the United Kingdom. Since US interests are disproportionately targeted by transnational terrorist groups, the United States expends the most proactive effort against these groups.[9]

There is one important consideration—namely, backlash—that curbs this underprovision of proactive measures. Backlash occurs when proactive efforts result in more grievances, and thus more terrorism, because of a public perception of excessive brutality on the part of the government.[10] When US drone strikes miss their targets and kill innocent people or otherwise result in collateral death, the resulting public backlash can bolster terrorists' ability to recruit others to their cause. Thus, targeted governments must plan their proactive measures carefully to avoid backlash. The famous movie *The Battle of Algiers* shows how the Front de Libération Nationale (FLN) used its terrorist attacks to provoke a French overreaction in terms of torture, executions, and brutal tactics. This proactive overreaction lost the French government its support among the French residents in Algeria, the French people at home, and the world community. Ultimately, the FLN won its independence in 1962 through strategically induced backlash and not through a military defeat of a strong French military.[11]

Next, consider defensive measures in this same transnational terrorism setting of multiple targeted countries and common terrorist threats. Each country's defensive actions to harden and protect targets at home and to guard its borders make it more costly for the terrorists to attack the country's interests at home. Consequently, terrorist groups respond by seeking less-guarded, softer targets in other countries. Countries with the requisite resources engage in a defensive race to transfer as many terrorist attacks as possible to countries abroad.[12] This strategic response occurs even if defending

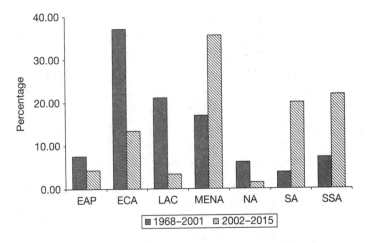

Figure 4.1 Regional distribution of transnational terrorist attacks, 1970–2001 and 2002–2015

countries' interests are attacked abroad, because the loss of assets abroad from terrorism is politically less costly than the same loss from terrorism at home. Thus, unlike proactive measures, defensive measures are likely to be overprovided.

To see the changing regional distribution of transnational terrorist attacks following enhanced post-9/11 security, consult Figure 4.1. In this figure, the regional classifications are those of the World Bank, which identifies seven regions: East Asia and Pacific, EAP; Europe and Central Asia, ECA; Latin America and the Caribbean, LAC; Middle East and North Africa, MENA; North America, NA; South Asia, SA; and sub-Saharan Africa, SSA. After 9/11, there were significant hardening of targets and borders in North America, Europe and Central Asia, and Latin America and the Caribbean. Figure 4.1 documents a large decline in the percentage of transnational terrorist attacks in these three regions. By contrast, there is a large percentage increase in transnational terrorist incidents in the Middle East and North Africa, South Asia, and sub-Saharan Africa, whose component countries have not greatly hardened targets or borders. Moreover, these regions

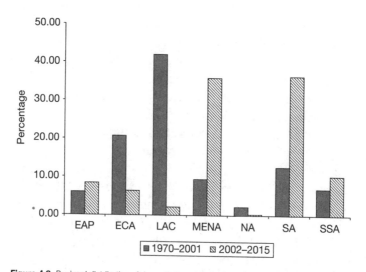

Figure 4.2 Regional distribution of domestic terrorist attacks, 1970–2001 and 2002–2015

are now home to numerous religious fundamentalist terrorist groups and contain many failed or weak states. Such states host numerous terrorist groups. Hence, it is not surprising that a similar transference of attacks characterizes the regional distribution of domestic terrorism after 2001, as shown in Figure 4.2.

Why Is Effective Counterterrorism More Difficult for Transnational Than for Domestic Terrorism?

There is an important, and easy to explain, asymmetry between the practice of proactive and defensive measures against transnational versus domestic terrorism.[13] For transnational terrorism, there is a strong motive to underspend on proactive measures and to overspend on defensive actions, so that we live in an overly guarded but dangerous world concerning transnational terrorism because terrorist resources are not sufficiently degraded. This follows because each country makes its counterterrorism decision without accounting for the benefits (in the case of proactive measures) or the costs (in the case of defensive actions) that its action or inaction confers on other targeted countries. This disregard for other countries is akin to overpolluting the global environment or to underproviding safeguards against infectious diseases.

By contrast, a country's domestic counterterrorism choices yield costs and benefits for only its own citizens. There are no spillovers of benefits or costs to other countries, since domestic terrorism consists of homegrown and home-directed attacks without consequences for other countries. Accordingly, the central government is best positioned and motivated to account for all of the benefits associated with its proactive measures against a domestic terrorist group. This government wants to degrade domestic terrorist groups so that all of its component states or provinces are made safer. Moreover, the central government has no incentive to transfer domestic terrorist attacks from one province to another through defensive efforts. This is precisely why the central government, and not a lower juris-diction, is charged with domestic counterterrorism decisions. The creation of the US Department of Homeland Security (DHS) was motivated to control terrorism at the central level and to coordinate counterterrorism policy among the various agencies of the federal government. Thus, with respect to do-mestic terrorism, we should not anticipate underprovision of proactive measures or overprovision of defensive measures by the central government.

There are many examples where countries rid themselves of terrorist groups that pose important domestic terrorism risks. Thus, Italy eliminated the Italian Red Brigades, Japan compromised Aum Shinrikyo, Belgium disbanded the Combatant Communist Cells, the Sri Lankan military defeated the Tamil Tigers, Peru ended the Shining Path, and France captured Direct Action members. Proactive measures are quite effective against domestic terrorists posing great threats to the host country. Such measures are much less effective against transnational terrorists holed up in remote areas in a failed state.[14]

Is There a Logical Sequence to the Application of Proactive and Defensive Measures?

Thus far, I have separately examined the application and effectiveness of the broad classes of defensive and proactive counterterrorism efforts against the two forms of terrorism. But, in fact, countries must either apply both measures together or sequentially. When they are sequenced, it makes sense to apply the proactive measure first in order to degrade the terrorist risk before making alternative defensive decisions.[15] This follows because once the terrorist risk is abated through offensive actions, the need for defensive effort is diminished. Effective proactive or preemptive measures limit the need for the ongoing period-to-period defensive response. If, for instance, no proactive measures are ever taken, then defensive expense must remain the same or increase, since the terrorist group's resources stay intact.

The precise amounts of the two measures to apply to the terrorist risk depend on the comparative costs of the two measures and the actions taken by other targeted countries. That is, proactive measures taken by one targeted country limit the need for such actions by other countries against the same threat. Moreover, these other targeted countries can reduce their level of defense in response to some country's proactive response against the common terrorist threat.

Are There Other Forms of Transference of Attacks?

I have only discussed defense-based transference of attacks from one targeted country to another when countries independently secure their borders. There are, however, other forms of transference.[16] Terrorist attacks can involve four general types of targets: official, military, business, and private parties. Official targets refer to government personnel, government offices, embassies, and police; military targets correspond to the National Guard, military bases, and military personnel; business targets are business personnel and assets; and private parties denote all other targets. Research shows that terrorists first concentrated their attacks in the late 1960s and early 1970s on government officials with whom they had grievances. Thus, terrorists initially attacked those individuals who could change policies to satisfy terrorists' demands. As potential official targets were hardened, terrorists transferred many of their attacks to business and private parties. During the 1970s, terrorists favored business attacks over those against private parties, which is also in accordance with the dominant leftist terrorists' anticapitalist orientation. As business targets were hardened, terrorists transferred some of their attacks to private parties. Military targets have always been a small share of attacks since these targets are fortified.

In regard to transnational terrorist attacks, the cumulative total of attacks against private parties surpassed those against business personnel in 1980. By 1999, total attacks against private parties overtook those against officials. Because private parties are the most difficult to protect, they are now the target of choice (opportunity), as recent terrorist attacks in Nice, Istanbul, Brussels, Paris, London, Manchester, Edmonton, New York, and elsewhere illustrate. This same hardening-induced target transference characterizes domestic terrorist attacks, except that the overtaking among target types is much quicker, as domestic groups more easily mimic other groups' targeting decisions.

Transference can also influence the mode of attacks. For example, as skyjackings became more difficult owing to metal detectors, terrorists substituted other types of hostage-taking missions, such as kidnappings. In addition, as the US government better secured its embassies, terrorists turned to the assassination of embassy officials outside of secured compounds. Thus, assassinations of embassy officials were substituted for armed attacks and bombings of US embassies. Such outcomes indicate that authorities must take precautions against policy-induced transference of attack types.[17] Transference is advantageous to society if it involves less-harmful attacks, which has not always been the case. In the latter regard, the introduction of metal detectors increased terrorist incidents with casualties by over twelve attacks per quarter in the long run.[18] Remember that skyjackings prior to 9/11 generally resulted in few or no casualties, which was not the case for armed attacks and bombings. When evaluating the net payoff of, say, metal detectors, researchers must account for these bothersome transferences. In the case of metal detectors, they were also deployed to guard embassies, thereby reducing embassy takeovers and attacks. Thus, metal detectors resulted in both harmful and beneficial consequences in terms of other modes of attack.

Are There Other Means of Counterterrorism?

There are some forms of counterterrorism that do not fit neatly into the proactive or defensive distinction. One such measure is to supply state-provided social services as a means to break the grip that some religious fundamentalist groups exercise over their members (see chapter 3).[19] Terrorist groups such as Hamas and Hezbollah offer much-needed social services to members and their families in return for members' loyalty and participation, which may even include engaging in suicide attacks. Without alternative sources for these services, recruits can be lured rather cheaply to the terrorist group. Once they are recruited, the terrorist group can withhold these services from the family of the operative if he or she does not carry out an assigned mission. Israeli efforts to cut off Palestinians from jobs in Israel paved the way for some terrorist groups to fill a void and offer social services.

Another line of research shows that conciliatory actions by the government may raise the anticipated payoff of nonterrorist protests, thereby curtailing the vicious cycle of violence. For the periods covering the First Intifada (1987–1993), the Oslo Lull (1993–2000), and the Second Intifada (2000–2004), an associated study finds that terrorism in Israel was abated following a large number of conciliatory acts by the Israeli government. Moreover, Israel-imposed indiscriminate punitive acts, which also raised the cost of terrorism, did not have an intended terror-reducing effect. Such studies indicate that actions to ratchet down the tension and violence may have a peace-inducing payoff.[20]

Do Retaliatory Raids Work to Curb Terrorism?

Just before midnight on April 14, 1986, eighteen US F-111 fighter-bombers took off from British airbases in Lakenheath and Upper Heyford to fly 2,800 nautical miles to conduct a retaliatory raid on Libya for its alleged involvement in the La Belle Discotheque bombing in West Berlin on April 4, 1986. The discotheque blast killed 3, including 2 US servicemen, and injured 231 others, including 62 Americans. In the early morning of April 15, fifteen A-6 and A-7 navy fighters left the decks of the USS *American* and the USS *Coral Sea*, two aircraft carriers in the Mediterranean Sea, to join in a bombing raid that included targets in Tripoli and Benghazi. Among the five targets was the Azizyah barracks in Tripoli, which at the time served as a residence for Muammar Gaddafi. During the raid, the barracks was heavily damaged, leaving Gaddafi's adopted one-year-old daughter dead and two of his sons injured. The other four targets included the Jamahiriyah barracks in Benghazi, the Sidi Bilal port west of Tripoli, the military portion of the Tripoli airport, and the Benina military airfield.[21]

One study examines the postraid deterrent effects on terrorist attacks leveled on US and UK targets. These two countries' terrorist attacks are singled out for study because they were the only countries associated with the raid. In fact,

France and Spain had denied US planes overflight rights during and after the mission. The Libyan raid had the unintended immediate consequence of greatly increasing terrorist attacks against the United States, the United Kingdom, and the rest of the world, but two-thirds of the increase was directed at the two complicitous countries. Within six months, these US- and UK-directed attacks began falling precipitously; within a year or so, the number of these attacks had returned to its preraid average value.[22] The immediate increase in attacks reflected terrorist backlash as attacks planned for the future were moved into the present to decry the US raid. Having expended their future resource pools, terrorists had to replenish their resources, thus resulting in a large decline in US-UK terrorist attacks some six months later. The crucial insight is that this raid had no lasting effect. A subsequent study on a number of Israeli retaliatory raids on Palestinian targets finds the same precise pattern: an immediate increase in terrorist attacks, followed by a lull and an eventual return to the preraid average number of attacks.[23]

Generally, one-time retaliatory raids are not effective. In contrast, the long-term "war on terror" after 9/11 took an immediate toll on al-Qaeda as it lost fighters and leaders. Moreover, al-Qaeda had to find new sources of financing. Eventually, even al-Qaeda recovered as it moved operations to other parts of the world and new groups joined the al-Qaeda brand.[24]

To engage in a sustained war on terror, a country must view the terrorist threat as sufficiently dire. For 9/11, the death toll exceeded any other foreign attack on US soil, even that of the Japanese attack on Pearl Harbor. Thus, the United States was prepared to lead a terrorism-motivated conflict in Afghanistan in October 2001. Some seventeen years later, US troops are still in Afghanistan. Despite concerted US efforts in Afghanistan, Iraq, Syria, Yemen, and elsewhere, terrorism continues to pose a security challenge to the United States and other countries that absorbs tens of billions of dollars in both defensive and proactive measures.

Can Foreign Aid Be Used to Effectively Address Terrorism?

Following 9/11, the Bush administration increased its foreign aid in the hopes of reducing terrorism.[25] Some of this aid took the form of military assistance to eradicate a recipient country's resident terrorist group; for example, US aid flowed to Pakistan to weaken the Taliban, al-Qaeda, and other resident terrorist groups. Recipients of US aid to fight terrorism at home often confront an incentive dilemma. If the recipient country uses the aid to rid itself of the resident terrorist group, then the aid will dry up. Thus, the aid recipient is motivated to appear to be fighting terrorism, but is not motivated to accomplish the task. This perverse incentive is known as a *moral hazard* problem, in which the donor and recipient countries' interests are not aligned. Moreover, the true actions of the recipient country are hidden from the donor, so that the recipient can claim that it is trying hard to defeat the terrorists, who are stronger than originally thought. Then the recipient appeals for more aid that it may have no intention of using against the terrorist group. In the case of Pakistan, the Musharraf regime did little to use US aid to weaken the Taliban during 2001–2008. Similar situations occurred in Afghanistan and Yemen. In fact, one fascinating study shows empirically that US counterterrorism aid increased the survival of the resident terrorist groups from 4.69 to 7.82 years, a 67 percent increase![26] This is surely a depressing, but understandable, finding; it cautions governments to understand the stakeholders' incentives associated with governmental policies.

Aid can also be used to alleviate poverty, which is a good thing in its own right. However, I showed in chapter 2 that poverty is not a cause of transnational terrorism. Given the above moral hazard problem and the absence of a terrorism-poverty linkage, I am not sanguine that foreign aid is an effective counterterrorism tool.

What Is the General Prognosis for International Cooperation?

For transnational terrorism, there is a proclivity for countries that are targeted by the same terrorist groups to underspend on proactive measures and overspend on defensive action. There are, therefore, grounds for countries to act cooperatively to address these inappropriate responses. After a major incident, such as 9/11, that underscores the exigency of transnational terrorism, there have ensued increased proactive efforts for countries to work in concert. In response to 9/11, the NATO alliance invoked Article 5 of its founding treaty for the first time, branding the incident as an attack on all member states, thus necessitating a collective response. This resulted in a multicountry invasion of Afghanistan, with many countries lending logistical support to the main combatant countries. In response to recent ISIS attacks and threats, the United States, the United Kingdom, Australia, France, and regional Middle Eastern powers have launched airstrikes in Iraq and Syria, while other countries have helped this proactive effort in other ways. If, therefore, the terrorism threat is perceived as sufficiently dire, then some proactive cooperation will occur. Nevertheless, this cooperation is still insufficient because of the strong pull on many countries to free ride on the efforts of the strong and those countries that are most threatened by ISIS.

There is, however, little cooperation in curbing overspending on defensive measures, intended to deflect potential terrorist attacks to other, less-secure countries. This absence of cooperation follows because countries want complete autonomy over how they fortify their own borders. In this regard, the one hopeful exception is the increasing adoption of the International Criminal Police Organization (Interpol) surveillance system, known as the Mobile Interpol Network Database (MIND) and the Fixed Interpol Network Database (FIND). The system became operational at the end of 2005. MIND/

FIND surveillance permits countries to screen passports and other documents at entry points against extensive, up-to-date Interpol databases on suspected terrorists, known fugitives, missing persons, and stolen and lost travel documents. For MIND, screened documents are instantaneously checked for matches in a locally stored copy of the Interpol databases that are downloaded every forty-eight hours. For FIND, scanned information is transmitted through the portal to Interpol headquarters in Lyon, France, to check for matches. The whole process takes a second or two. The number of countries installing MIND/FIND increased from a handful in 2005 to well over a hundred in 2012. Moreover, research shows that this surveillance system is tied to fewer transnational terrorist incidents each year among those countries that systemically use MIND/FIND. Another investigation of Interpol counterterrorism efforts indicates a payback of US$40 to US$200 per dollar spent, depending on alternative counterfactual assumptions.[27] Thus, there are some hopeful signs of cooperation among governments despite myriad impediments. In chapter 5, I examine international cooperation among sovereign governments from another vantage in order to explain why terrorist groups have achieved greater cooperation than targeted countries.

Are UN Conventions and Resolutions Effective against Terrorism?

UN conventions are formal agreements or treaties among ratifying countries that mandate some action. By contrast, UN resolutions are stated views or decisions of ratifying countries, recognizing an issue of concern. Although UN conventions are binding on ratifying countries, there is no explicit enforcement mechanism, thus leaving some countries to ignore the mandate.

Since the early 1960s, there have been many conventions and resolutions by the United Nations and other multilateral institutions to ban particular acts of terrorism. Most notably, the International Civil Aviation Organization (ICAO) issued a convention banning hijackings on December 16, 1970, which entered into force on October 14, 1971.[28] Prior to the issuance of this ICAO convention, UN General Assembly Resolution 2551 in December 1969 and UN General Assembly Resolution 2645 in November 1970 outlawed hijackings. On February 29, 1977, a UN convention protecting diplomatic and other protected persons entered into force. Another UN convention outlawed hostage taking on June 3, 1983. Terrorist bombings were later banned by a UN convention on May 23, 2001, followed by a convention suppressing the financing of terrorism on April 10, 2002.

Some terrorist experts and government officials view UN conventions as an effective counterterrorism tool.[29] Unfortunately, the record indicates otherwise. Empirical studies show that past multilateral organizations' and UN resolutions and conventions have had no measurable effect on particular banned terrorist practices.[30] For example, the quarterly average number of hostage-taking incidents was the same before and after the convention banning hostage taking went into effect. This was also the case for hijackings, bombings, and crimes against protected persons in light of their respective conventions. Surely part of the problem is the absence of any enforcement mechanism to impose punishment on violators or sponsoring states. Any action must come from a country that has been disproportionately harmed by an outlawed terrorist practice. Terrorists purposely operate in weak states and inaccessible places to elude such retribution.

Can International Efforts Limit Terrorist Financing?

Following 9/11, many countries were intent on curtailing terrorist financial assets in numerous ways: identifying and closing charities with terrorist links; identifying and seizing terrorists' funds in the banking system; and curbing terrorists' abilities to launder funds. Just before 9/11, the Egmont Group (an international cooperative body) encouraged national financial intelligence units (FIUs) to exchange information in an effort to reduce the financial resources of terrorists. Moreover, the Financial Action Task Force on Money Laundering (FATF), a G-7 advisory group, issued new recommendations after 9/11 to reduce terrorist financing. In September 2003, the US Treasury reported that $135 million of alleged terrorists' assets had been frozen worldwide after 9/11. The White House increased this figure to $200 million in February 2004. Thus, initial international cooperation on this front took place and stressed terrorist operations.[31]

Unfortunately, the terrorists developed ways around these efforts by hiding money in noncompliant countries, trading in precious commodities, using the hawala system of informal cash transfers, disguising transactions through legitimate business dealings, and capturing hostages for ransoms. This list is by no means exhaustive. The hawala system masks transfers through the settlement of bookkeeping balances among a network of balance holders at a later time through a wire transfer or an exchange of commodities. In the process, the identity of the transferors and the amount of the transfer are masked from the authorities.[32]

These actions demonstrate that terrorist groups are a "moving target" that takes evasive actions with respect to international cooperative attempts to cut their funding. Such international cooperation works in the short run, but loses its effectiveness over time as terrorists develop new sources of financing.[33] In the case of ISIS, the group extorted money from populations under its control and profited from seized oil fields.[34] Given that most terrorist operations are inexpensive, terrorists can often circumvent concerted efforts to stem their financing in rather short order.

Is Information Adequately Shared among Countries in the Fight against Terrorism?

This is a difficult question to answer because the sharing of intelligence concerning terrorism is classified. Hence, I can only speculate on this answer based on what I hear in the news. Like other security concerns, countries are loath to share information that may compromise their actions or sources. This became clear when the United Kingdom voiced its displeasure with the Trump administration for revealing the identity of the Manchester Arena suicide bomber before the British authorities had completed its arrest of suspects and potential accomplices. Apparently, this identity had been revealed to US authorities in the normal course of sharing intelligence. The United States and the United Kingdom have had a long-standing practice of sharing intelligence on terrorism. This is surely true of other NATO allies. In the US DHS, the Department of Analysis and Operations gathers intelligence and interfaces with other components of DHS and lower levels of the US government. The Department of Analysis and Operations also interfaces with the international intelligence community and includes the Office of Intelligence and Analysis.[35]

At times, countries' private agendas may limit or even cut off intelligence sharing. Given US alliance with the Iraqi Kurds in the fight against ISIS, any intelligence sharing between the United States and Turkey these days is likely extremely limited. This follows because the current Turkish regime views the Kurds as a terrorist threat. There are other instances within NATO where countries' interests may clash with respect to sharing intelligence on terrorism. Germany and Turkey may be another example.

Since countries are unlikely to be as motivated to protect other countries' interests, even those of friends, to the same extent that they guard their own interests, I would surmise that intelligence is inadequately shared among countries.

This should not be surprising insofar as the *9/11 Commission Report* indicated that intelligence on terrorism was very poorly shared among US government agencies prior to the 9/11 attack. This lack of coordination, in part, motivated the creation of DHS.[36]

Should Concessions Be Made to Terrorist Kidnappers?

During 1982–1992, Hezbollah (also known at the time as Islamic Jihad) relied on kidnappings in Beirut to obtain ransoms and political concessions. This terrorist group sought out soft targets that included academics, journalists, and businessmen. The negotiated releases of Rev. Benjamin Weir (in September 1985), Rev. Lawrence Jenco (in July 1986), and David Jacobsen (in November 1986) were subsequently followed by the abduction of Robert Polhill, Alan Steen, and Jesse Turner on January 24, 1987. These three academics were employed at the time by Beirut University College. Their replacement for the earlier released hostages was highly publicized when it became known that the Reagan administration had traded arms for hostages to secure the freedom of Weir, Jenco, and Jacobsen.[37] The trade resulted in the "Irangate" scandal. The Reagan administration had broken its no-concession pledge as it sought the release of these three hostages and that of a fourth American hostage—William Buckley—a Central Intelligence Agency (CIA) officer who, unbeknownst to the United States, had already been murdered by his captors.

This exchange illustrates some essential insights about making concessions to terrorist kidnappers. First, many governments will renege on their no-concession pledge if sufficiently valuable hostages are taken. For instance, Israeli premier Golda Meir appeared prepared to meet the terrorists' demands in return for the release of ninety schoolchildren taken hostage at Maalot on May 15, 1974. Second, the payment of ransoms often results in the abduction of additional hostages. Third, hostage takers tend to generalize from one government's action to that of other governments. Hence, as concessions were made by some governments during the Beirut kidnapping campaign, terrorists often turned to soft targets from other countries, so that one country's concessions tarnished the perceived reputation of other governments for maintaining their pledged no-concession stance.

Recent research examines whether a country's concessions to terrorists truly encourage additional kidnappings.[38] One investigation finds that past concessions made to terrorist kidnappers resulted in 2.62 additional abductions, which is a sobering finding. A more recent study distinguishes among countries that hold firm and those that more frequently grant concessions. The latter countries are dubbed concessionaire countries. During 2001–2013, terrorist negotiation successes encouraged 64 to 87 percent more kidnappings. Unlike concessionaires, countries that maintained their no-concession pledge did not experience an increase in their average number of abductions.

There is yet another rationale for holding firm since, by doing so, governments deprive terrorists of funds to support their operations, such as further kidnappings and other types of terrorist attacks. The *New York Times* reported that nearly $130 million had been paid to al-Qaeda and affiliates between 2008 and 2013, enough to have financed half of these groups' operations.[39] The unmistakable message is that, if hostage taking is to become less desirable for the terrorists, governments must hold firm and not concede ransoms despite the horrific consequences to the hostages.

How Has the Department of Homeland Security Contributed to Counterterrorism?

Following 9/11, there was a greater apparent need in the United States for more interagency communication and coordination. This recognition led to the creation of the DHS in 2002 as a means to eliminate waste and foster synergy among component agencies at all jurisdictional levels.[40] The DHS represented a bold initiative to make America safer from the threat of terrorism.

If the DHS was meant to combine all US agencies charged with counterterrorism under one umbrella department, then it is fair to point out some essential agencies are missing, such as the Federal Bureau of Investigation (FBI) and the CIA. The former is concerned with thwarting domestic terrorism, and the latter is concerned with thwarting transnational terrorism. Thus, there may remain significant communication and coordination issues despite the DHS mandate. In particular, the DHS is primarily charged with defensive policies, while the FBI, CIA, and Department of Defense (DOD) are involved with proactive policies. The DHS does not really allow for coordination between the two types of counterterrorism actions, so that overspending on defensive measures and underspending on proactive measures are not addressed. On a more positive note, the DHS does address a wide range of counterterrorism concerns that include first responders, local grants, antibiotic and antidote stockpiling, transportation security, border protection, and immigration and customs enforcement.

5

ASYMMETRIES AND TERRORISM

Why Are Asymmetries Important for Terrorism?

At 11:18 a.m. on October 12, 2000, a small fiberglass boat sped toward the port side of the USS *Cole*, moored for a routine fuel stop at Aden harbor in Yemen. On the *Cole*'s deck, navy sailors with guns failed to fire at the fast-approaching boat because the US Navy's strict rules of engagement forbid sailors from firing unless fired upon. The small boat contained two suicide terrorists and four hundred to seven hundred pounds of explosives that blasted a forty- by sixty-foot hole in the ship's hull, killing seventeen sailors and injuring thirty-nine. It took the ship's crew three days to contain the flooding in the engine rooms and to secure the ship. Despite the huge port-side gash, the keel was undamaged, meaning that the ship was repairable. On October 29, the USS *Cole* was loaded onto a huge Norwegian transport ship, the *Blue Marlin*, to be carried back to the United States. Repairs eventually cost $240 million.[1]

This horrible incident underscores a number of asymmetries that plague governments' efforts to address terrorism. First, the navy ship was particularly vulnerable because it obeyed rules of engagement, while the terrorists followed no rules of engagement. Accordingly, the plot carried out by al-Qaeda on the USS *Cole* was hugely successful. Following this incident, the US Navy altered its rules of engagement, allowing armed guards to fire on potential threats. Second, the cost of the bomb and dinghy was minuscule, while the damage to the ship was huge, tens of thousands times that incurred in materials to the perpetrators. Third, the terrorists had all of the time necessary to identify the *Cole*'s greatest vulnerability, while the navy guards had almost no time to assess and react to the threat. Fourth, the loss of life among the sailors was greater than that among the terrorists. Fifth, such attacks make it difficult for the well-identified victim to identify the perpetrator in order to deliver a retaliatory response.

Throughout this chapter, myriad asymmetries are identified between terrorists and their government adversary. In most cases, these asymmetries confer an advantage to the terrorists over their much stronger government adversary. Terrorists are masters at exploiting and, in many instances, creating these asymmetries to promote their political agenda. Effective counterterrorism policy requires actions to reduce these asymmetries. To really understand terrorism, one must gain an appreciation for how terrorists can be so effective with so few resources over such a formidable government opponent.

What Is Asymmetric Warfare and How Does It Apply to Terrorism?

After the collapse of the Soviet Union, the United States assumed the status of the sole superpower. As such, its military planners in the Department of Defense (DOD) started to contemplate asymmetric warfare, as the United States would confront much weaker conventional and nonconventional opponents in the future. Nonconventional adversaries may involve terrorist groups, insurgents, drug cartels, rogue states, failed states, and cybercriminals. Certainly, asymmetric warfare between superior and inferior adversaries is not new. The Assassins waged an asymmetric war during 1090–1275 CE against the Turkish Seljuk Empire in Persia and Syria, while the Zealots-Sicarii waged an asymmetric war during 66–73

CE against the Romans in Judea. During the post–Cold War era, rogue and failed states posed a security challenge to the United States. Rogue states, such as North Korea, that do not follow standard norms of behavior may present a threat from nuclear weapon proliferation; failed states, such as Somalia, Yemen, and Afghanistan, that cannot control their territory may present a threat from resident terrorist groups. Any confrontation between the United States and these states is very unbalanced. After 9/11, the DOD again focused on the notion of asymmetric warfare as it prepared to attack al-Qaeda and the Taliban, two much weaker opponents, on their home territory in Afghanistan.

Asymmetric warfare is difficult to define in a meaningful way because all wars that do not conclude in a stalemate must necessarily have involved unequal belligerents. Moreover, asymmetry in warfare may concern many dimensions— information, weapon technology, force size, manpower, tactics, resources, timing, and others. One could argue that asymmetric warfare is a meaningless concept because it applies in virtually all situations. I do not ascribe to this view and appreciate that asymmetries may differ greatly. Moreover, the extent of asymmetry often tells us much about the tactics of the adversaries. For example, less asymmetry among opponents should result in more conventional warfare. I offer the following definition: *asymmetric warfare* involves conflict between two unevenly matched adversaries, who often employ different tactics to protect their own weaknesses and to circumvent their adversary's strength.[2]

My asymmetric warfare definition is reminiscent of Sun Tzu's ancient treatise on military tactics, dating back to the fifth century BCE. His book, *The Art of War*, consists of thirteen chapters, each indicating strategic war-fighting principles such as limiting the cost of warfare, minimizing direct confrontation with the enemy, and defending positions against the enemy. A key tactical lesson of Sun Tzu is to take advantage of an enemy's strength, while attacking its weakness. In the assault on the USS *Cole*, the ship's imposing high profile allowed the dinghy to approach most of the way undetected. Since the ship is most vulnerable when being refueled, the terrorists attacked the ship's greatest weakness, fostered by the navy's rules of engagement. Time and again, terrorists plan their missions to exploit their enemy's strength, while attacking its weakness, so that the notion of asymmetric warfare aptly applies to terrorism. Given this realization, the authorities must put themselves in the terrorists' place and ask how their greatest strengths can be exploited through new innovations of the terrorists.

Why Are Terrorist Groups Better Able to Cooperate Than Targeted Governments?

One of the most fundamental asymmetries between governments and terrorists concerns terrorists' long-standing ability to cooperate and governments' general failure to cooperate. The latter is even true of governments targeted by the same terrorist groups. In chapters 1 and 4, I show that governments' independently chosen defensive and offensive measures are not ideal for confronting a common transnational terrorist threat. In particular, governments spend too much on defense and too little on offense. Thus, governments can achieve gains by working together when deciding counterterrorism choices, but they seldom do so.

From the late 1960s, terrorist groups have shared personnel, intelligence, logistics, innovations, training camps, and resources. The Palestinian terrorists (for example, the Popular Front for the Liberation of Palestine [PFLP]) worked together with the Provisional Irish Republican Army (PIRA), the Japanese Red Army, the German Revolutionary Cells, and other European leftist groups in the late 1960s, 1970s, and 1980s. The infamous hijacking of Air France Flight 139, en route from Athens to Paris on June 27, 1976, was a joint operation carried out initially by two PFLP and two Revolutionary

Cells hijackers. The plane was eventually diverted to the Entebbe airport in Uganda, where four additional hijackers joined the team. The hijackers demanded the release of fifty-three terrorists imprisoned in Israel, Switzerland, West Germany, France, and Kenya, including prominent members of the German-based Red Army Faction (initially known as the Baader-Meinhof Group). Operation Thunderbolt, engineered by Israeli commandos, ended the incident with the deaths of three hostages in the raid.[3]

More recently, al-Qaeda forged a loosely tied network of affiliated terrorist groups. Osama bin Laden began franchising other Islamic fundamentalist groups. Most significantly, al-Qaeda provided an identifying and unifying brand that mushroomed in importance following the success of 9/11. Today, al-Qaeda-affiliated groups include the al-Nusra Front, Boko Haram, Islamic State in Iraq and Syria (ISIS), al-Shabaab, al-Qaeda in the Arabian Peninsula (AQAP), al-Qaeda in the Islamic Maghreb (AQAP), Jemaah Islamiyah, Islamic Movement of Uzbekistan (IMU), and many others scattered throughout the world.[4]

So why do terrorists succeed so much better than governments in forging truly cooperative links? There are at least four reasons. First, governments put great weight on exercising autonomy over their security matters. They carefully guard their intelligence and its sources from other countries, partly to avoid compromising such sources. In contrast, terrorist groups place less weight on autonomy when other groups are confronting the same enemy and seeking complementary goals—for example, attacking American interests.[5]

Second, terrorist groups are more inclined to cooperate because of their relative weakness compared with their well-armed and formidable government adversary. Given their relatively modest resources, terrorist groups have little choice but to pool their resources in order to present a greater threat. By contrast, the large arsenal and resource pools of many governments mean that they have less need to cooperate with other targeted governments, particularly because such cooperation sacrifices autonomy.

Third, terrorists agree on who are their enemies, such as the United States, the United Kingdom, France, and Israel, while governments do not always concur on what groups are terrorists. For instance, the European Union did not consider Hamas to be a terrorist group for many years. Sharing some common foes, terrorist groups can see the benefit from coordinating operations with other terrorist groups. In some instances, this coordination is more tacit than explicit, as when many terrorist groups simultaneously strike US targets. Such a spate of attacks followed the US retaliatory raid on Libya on April 15, 1986, and also the start of the first Gulf War, known as Desert Storm, on January 17, 1991. The US-led Desert Storm was in reaction to Iraq's invasion of Kuwait.

Fourth, by being tenured for life, terrorist leaders view intergroup interactions as continual. This, in turn, allows them to overcome the incentive to renege on promised support to another leader, thereby escaping a potential prisoner's dilemma. For such dilemmas, cooperation might be withheld after receiving it from their counterpart if leaders think that other leaders cannot subsequently punish them for their infidelity. When group interactions are continual, a tit-for-tat punishment can be applied when a group's failure to deliver its promised support is subsequently met with the double-crossed group withholding its pledged cooperation. The tit-for-tat punishment ends once the reneging group begins to deliver its promised cooperation. By contrast, democratically elected leaders' interests in the future are limited by the length of the election cycle and their likelihood of being re-elected. Agreement between countries to combat terrorism in concert may be rather short-lived if governments change or are about to change (a lame-duck administration). For instance, the new Spanish prime minister José Luis Rodriguez Zapatero pulled Spanish troops out of US-led operations in Iraq after his victory in the national elections. This withdrawal followed from the terrorists linking their Madrid commuter train bombings on March 11, 2004, as retribution for Spanish support for the US-led war on terror. Government leaders' short-term viewpoint limits transnational counterterrorism cooperation because tit-for-tat punishment loses its efficacy when a successor leader no longer feels bound by the predecessor's agreement. Any transnational agreement between governments must have a permanency that transcends a change in government. And such permanency is very difficult to achieve in counterterrorism agreements, especially when sticking to the agreement carries cost, as in the case of Spain after the March 11, 2004, attack and the terrorists' promise of future attacks in Spain.

Who Are Better Informed about Their Adversaries?

By their nature, terrorist groups are covert. The maintenance of secrecy with respect to their size, location, planned operations, tactics, and organizational structure is necessary for their survival. As a consequence, countries are not well informed about terrorist groups' strength, whereas terrorist groups can easily discover how many governmental resources are allocated to some, but not all, forms of counterterrorism. In the United States, the Department of Homeland Security's (DHS's) budget is a matter of public record, and this budget is surprisingly detailed in its breakdown, including even how much is spent on air marshals. However, a country's spending on some offensive measures, such as gathering intelligence or drone strikes, is not readily known by the public or terrorist groups. Thus, asymmetric information, where one adversary is more informed than the other, certainly characterizes terrorist groups and their targeted countries to varying degrees depending on the particular bit of sought-after information.

This asymmetric information is aptly illustrated by US estimates of the size of al-Qaeda in Afghanistan as "several hundred to several thousand members," reported by the US Department of State just five months prior to 9/11.[6] Not only is this estimate wide in its range, but it is also inaccurate. After the start of the US invasion of Afghanistan on October 7, 2001, the United States re-estimated this figure to be well over ten thousand. Such misleading US intelligence not only hampered the planning of military operations, but the underestimation also inhibited US efforts to convince other countries to contribute troops and supplies to defeat al-Qaeda and the Taliban.

Terrorists exploit government's ignorance about their strength or size for strategic purposes. In particular, a terrorist group may feint strength with large-scale attacks using most of its resources, thereby leaving few resources for other immediate operations. Such action by the group is to make the government falsely view the group as strong so that the government grants concessions to curtail future attacks. In other instances, the terrorist group may deceive with small-scale attacks so that the government is later surprised by a large-scale, devastating attack. Adversarial size is, perhaps, the most important thing to know and is generally better known by the terrorists than the government.[7]

What Target Asymmetries Are Associated with Terrorism?

The choice of targeting implies some interesting asymmetries that involve asymmetric information. Countries are target-rich, with potential targets at public events, commercial ventures, government buildings, public places, or just about anywhere. In contrast, terrorist groups are made target-poor by locating in inaccessible places, such as the caves of Afghanistan, dense jungle retreats, or mountainous hideaways. At other times, terrorists go to the opposite extreme and hide in plain sight in densely populated urban areas so that any preemptive attack by the government results in unacceptable collateral casualties. On this targeting dimension, terrorists are advantaged over governments.

Another targeting asymmetry that favors the terrorists over the government is nicely illustrated by the PIRA bombing of the

Grand Hotel, the Tory conference venue, in Brighton, England, on October 12, 1984. The nine-kilo bomb was intended to assassinate Prime Minister Margaret Thatcher and her entire cabinet and was planted under the bathroom floor of Room 629. Thatcher was the occupant of this room. The bomb exploded at 2:54 a.m., just after Mrs. Thatcher had left the bathroom. The blast killed five and injured thirty-three, but none of the dead included cabinet members. Following the incident and Thatcher's narrow escape, a statement from the IRA said, "Today, we were unlucky. But remember we have to be lucky once. You will have to be lucky always." This famous, often-quoted statement eloquently summarizes an asymmetry favoring the terrorists.[8]

The subsequent forensic investigation of the bombing found that Patrick Joseph Magee had checked into the hotel a month before the planned Tory conference. He planted the bomb and had set it to explode twenty-four days, six hours, and thirty-five minutes later, at a time when conference delegates would be asleep. Apparently, the preconference surveillance of the hotel venue did not start until a few weeks before the conference, so that Magee could plant the bomb without raising suspicions by checking into the hotel before the surveillance started. His action points to another targeting asymmetry. Governments must guard everywhere, while terrorists can identify and attack soft targets, whose destruction creates the greatest cost to society.

Are There Cost Asymmetries between Terrorists and Governments?

There are at least two noteworthy cost asymmetries, both of which strongly favor the terrorists over a vigilant government. Since the latter must protect innumerable potential targets, defensive measures are very expensive. Given limited funds, governments must keep costs within budgetary constraints by protecting the most valuable, likely, and vulnerable targets. Consequently, many targets must go unprotected, thereby opening them up to attack. The terrorists apply their limited resources wisely by concentrating on a few targets. Terrorists first examine potential targets to ascertain their vulnerability and likely payoff. Once the target is chosen, the terrorists enter the planning stage, wherein they assign the minimum resources necessary for a successful operation. Lastly, they execute the mission. Given all of the possible targets, the authorities are often caught unaware.

The overwhelming message is that terrorists possess a real resource advantage because they need to commit relatively few resources compared to their government adversary. This results in a second cost asymmetry that favors the terrorists. Consider a suicide bombing: A terrorist suicide vest costs about $150 but can kill many and wreak millions of dollars in damages. Typically, the "damage exchange rate" (DER) greatly favors the terrorists. For a given attack, this rate measures how many dollars of damage result from each dollar of attack expenditure. For 9/11, the terrorists' cost of the attack was under $500,000 and the ensuing damage was conservatively estimated at $84 billion, resulting in a DER of 168,000 to 1. Other landmark attacks have the following estimated DERs: Madrid train bombings, 26,900 to 1; the USS *Cole*, 24,440 to 1; the Bali nightclub bombings (October 12, 2002), 60,000 to 1; and the London transport bombings (July 7, 2005), 1,270,000 to 1.[9] In most daily endeavors, including investment opportunities, payoff rates are nowhere as large as those of these attacks. Many other large-scale terrorist incidents have similarly large DERs. Rates are high because most terrorist attacks are relatively cheap to execute and can result in high property and personal cost. Even small bombings have DERs that are large because bombs are very inexpensive compared to the property damage that they cause.

Is There a Timing Asymmetry?

Generally, the government acts first and applies its defensive resources so as to fortify the most vulnerable and valued potential targets. After observing this allocation, the terrorist group moves second and decides what target offers the greatest anticipated payoff in terms of damage. As such damages mount, the besieged government is under greater pressure to concede to some demands of the terrorists. However, is there a necessary first- or second-mover advantage in terrorism?

Let's take a step back and begin by considering the notion of first- and second-mover advantage, which is a game-theoretic concept. When I teach this concept, I ask my students for a show of hands as to whether it is better to move first or second. Many more than half feel that there is always an advantage to moving first. I then ask one of these students to play Rock-Paper-Scissors with me and tell the student to move first and show me his or her choice. I then choose second and win. In chess, the consensus is that there is a slight first-mover advantage. There is a definite first-mover advantage in Tic-Tac-Toe, since moving first and putting the X in the middle square ensures at least a tie. In elections, there is usually a second-mover advantage, because knowing the opponent's platform allows a candidate to propose a platform that defeats the revealed platform by matching popular positions and opposing unpopular ones. Thus, there is little wonder why many candidates today reveal little of their views on issues and rather focus on destroying their opponent's character. The general principle is that a first-mover advantage exists when commitment is advantageous, while a second-mover advantage exists when flexibility is advantageous.[10]

Generally speaking, being able to observe fortification choices of the government provides a second-mover advantage to the terrorists. *Flexibility* in target selection is advantageous. Governments can counter this second-mover advantage to some extent by greatly fortifying the most important targets and clearly indicating their fortification choices, so that terrorists are guided to attack less-valuable targets. If, covertly, the government fortifies allegedly unprotected, but inviting, targets, then it may lay a trap for the terrorists. Even when this trap fails, the terrorists end up attacking less-damaging venues. Thus, the second-mover advantage of terrorists may be less than presupposed if defensive measures are made public.[11]

How Do Weakest-Link and Best-Shot Actions Influence Counterterrorism?

Many counterterrorism actions for a collective of countries can be largely undone by a single noncooperative country. Consider denying safe havens to terrorist groups. Even one or two countries that break from the others and provide safe haven may offset much of the efforts of those countries that do not offer sanctuary. These sanctuaries are often in failed or failing states that cannot eliminate resident terrorist groups. Denying safe haven is a weakest-link outcome, for which the least action determines the safety of all countries. Another weakest-link example is freezing terrorist assets or eliminating terrorist financing. The action of financial institutions in one or a few countries to launder terrorist funds may be sufficient to dilute the efforts of most countries to inhibit such laundering. This is particularly true because terrorist operations are relatively cheap, so that only modest financing is needed. Another weakest-link counterterrorism measure is adhering to a no-concession pledge with respect to ransom payment to terrorist kidnappers. As a country reneges on its pledge and pays a ransom, its payment makes terrorist groups doubt the pledge of the collective, especially if the "right" hostage is abducted. Moreover, paid ransoms finance terrorist operations, thereby putting other countries in jeopardy (see chapter 4). A ten-million-dollar ransom can fund lots of bombings. Weakest-link counterterrorism actions are particularly difficult to achieve, which greatly favors the terrorists.

By contrast, best-shot counterterrorism measures require only one capable country to act for the benefit of all. Typically, the most capable country should engage in the best-shot effort.

Limiting the actions of a state-sponsoring regime through a retaliatory raid, as done by the United States against Libya in April 1986, is best-shot retaliation. This retaliatory raid was in response to a Libyan-supported bombing in Berlin earlier in April 1986 that targeted a nightclub frequented by US service personnel. Following this raid, Libya curbed, but did not end, its state-sponsorship role. Gaining intelligence on a plot to bring down transatlantic commercial flights with liquid bombs was a best-shot action by the United Kingdom that benefited all countries in August 2006. Best-shot counterterrorism measures favor countries over the terrorists, especially if the capable best-shooter country is sufficiently motivated to act. Ironically, by focusing their attacks on US interests, terrorists put themselves in greater peril than had they spread their attacks over more countries. This follows because the United States is then more motivated to provide best-shot actions.[12]

From the terrorists' vantage, best-shot actions ensue when terrorists successfully create a new mode of attack, such as suicide car bombings in the 1980s and, more recently, the use of trucks to plow down pedestrians. These best-shot innovations are then imitated by other terrorist groups, thereby putting the public in great danger. With the Internet and modern media, such innovations can be spread to terrorist groups globally in a matter of days.

Is There an Identity Asymmetry?

Another informational asymmetry that favors terrorists over their government foes concerns identity. When governments engage in unpopular or grievance-creating policies, the involved officeholders are well known. If terrorists later choose to attack these decision-makers or their underlings, it is easy to know whom to target, though it is not always easy to confront the protected officials directly. However, their subordinates are easier to attack.

The identity of those responsible for a terrorist attack is more difficult to ascertain unless a *credible* claim of responsibility is issued or there is sufficient forensic evidence. For example, a long-term investigation eventually pinned the blame for the downing of Pan Am Flight 103 over Lockerbie, Scotland, in December 1988 on two Libyan intelligence agents. At one time in the investigation, it was strongly believed that the Popular Front for the Liberation of Palestine–General Command (PFLP-GC), a breakaway group from the PFLP, had manufactured the altitude bomb, set to explode at thirty-one thousand feet when the plane entered its cruising altitude in the Atlantic flight corridor. This belief was eventually dismissed owing to differences in the bomb aboard Flight 103 and those made by PFLP-GC. Moreover, Syria or Iran, which supported the PFLP-GC at the time, was falsely thought to have sponsored the downing of the airliner. This example aptly demonstrates that attributing blame for unclaimed terrorist attacks on responsible parties is not easy.[13]

Is There an Asymmetry in Restraint?

Today's religious fundamentalist terrorists are unrestrained in their violence, unlike leftist terrorists, who tried to minimize their brutality and limit collateral damage in order to maintain their constituency. Fundamentalist terrorists demonize nonfollowers and can be particularly bloodthirsty. Their suicide bombings do not discriminate among their victims. For example, three coordinated suicide bombings at hotels— the Radisson SAS, the Grand Hyatt, and the Days Inn—in Amman, Jordan, on November 9, 2005, by al-Qaeda in Iraq (the forerunner of ISIS) left 60 dead and 115 injured, mostly Muslims. The suicide bombing in the Philadelphia Ballroom of the Radisson SAS killed 38 in a wedding party. In a subsequent letter to Abu Musab al-Zarqawi, the then-leader of al-Qaeda in Iraq, Osama bin Laden complained that such attacks harmed the al-Qaeda brand.[14]

In contrast, governments must adhere to rules of law and show restraint in dealing with terrorists. This restraint can greatly advantage terrorists, as was the case with Aum Shinrikyo, which perpetrated the sarin attack on the Tokyo subway on the morning of March 20, 1995, which killed twelve and injured well over a thousand people. Despite earlier sarin and anthrax attacks, the Japanese authorities did not raid Aum Shinrikyo's headquarters until indisputable evidence surfaced that the group was planning more deadly future attacks to follow the sarin subway attack.

What Are the Organizational Asymmetries between Terrorist Groups and Governments?

In chapter 3, I touched on how terrorist groups organize themselves today into loosely tied networks, where one cell's members may be unaware of other cells' members. Here, I focus on organizational differences between governments and their terrorist adversaries. Governments are hierarchically organized with the executive branch at the pinnacle. In the United States, there are many parts of the executive branch with an antiterrorist role, including DHS, the Federal Bureau of Investigation (FBI), the Central Intelligence Agency (CIA), DOD, and others. After 9/11, the formation of DHS was designed, in part, to foster better cooperation and intelligence sharing among various components of the government tasked with countering terrorism. Although DHS accomplished much by bringing many parts of the US counterterrorism apparatus within the same department, crucial pieces, such as the CIA and FBI, were left out, which can result in duplication, wasteful spending, and possible blindsides. The hierarchical structure is helpful in having the central government coordinate counterterrorism efforts at the state level, and for the latter doing the same at the local level.

During much of the leftist or third-wave era of terrorism, terrorist groups were also hierarchically structured. Things

gradually changed with respect to the organizational structure of terrorist groups in the aftermath of the General James
Dozier rescue in 1982. Dozier had been the senior US officer at
NATO's southern Europe ground forces base in Verona, Italy.
He had been kidnapped by Italian Red Brigades (RB) terrorists
from his home on December 17, 1981, and held until his rescue
by a special police unit on January 28, 1982. As the authorities
searched for Dozier, they conducted raids on RB operatives
and their hideouts, constantly acquiring more information
on RB planned attacks, hideouts' locations, and membership.
The group's hierarchical and tightly knit structure meant that
captured members knew the identity of many other members.
When Dozier was freed unharmed, the police nabbed Antonio
Savasta at the scene. For an immunity pledge, consistent with
a district attorney's ploy to induce a confession in a prisoner's
dilemma, Savasta provided state's evidence that led to the
arrests of two hundred RB members. The subsequent trials
of arrested members effectively ended the RB and alerted
terrorists everywhere to the risks of tightly linked hierarchical
structures.[15]

Terrorist groups that later suffered a similar fate stemming
from their tightly linked structure include Aum Shinrikyo
in Japan, 17 November in Greece, and Direct Action in
France. Over time, terrorists developed loosely linked cells
that operated more or less autonomously, which resulted
in a trade-off between functionality and vulnerability (see
chapter 4).[16] Small autonomous cells could not always accomplish logistically complex missions. Even 9/11 suggests this.
The three five-man squads succeeded in crashing their planes
as planned, while the one four-man squad on United Airlines
Flight 93 was overwhelmed by the passengers and crashed in
a field in Shanksville, PA.[17] Terrorist groups' nonhierarchical
structures offer both a benefit and a cost to the authorities.
On one hand, the benefit derives from groups having to
concentrate on less ambitious missions with presumably
fewer casualties and less property damage. On the other

Welcome to Guthrie Memorial
Library: Hanover's Public Library
JAMES checked out the following
items:

1. **Dark sacred night**
   Barcode: 34007002337009
   Due: 12/12/2018
2. **City of devils : the two men
   who ruled the underworld
   of old Shanghai**
   Barcode: 33454005616537
   Due: 12/12/2018

Today's Date: 11/21/2018
You Saved $57.00 by borrowing
from the library!

hand, the terrorist groups are more immune to attack even when members are compromised. Consider Aum Shinrikyo, which manufactured VX and sarin gases and planned an air assault on Tokyo using an acquired Mi-17 helicopter, fitted with spraying equipment to kill tens of thousands on the ground with sarin gas.[18] This grand plan required the hierarchical structure that eventually did the group in. Among its members, Aum Shinrikyo had nuclear physicists working on developing radiological and nuclear bombs!

Is Size an Advantage for the Adversaries?

For terrorists, group size supports survival and visibility, as demonstrated in many recent empirical studies[19] and as previously mentioned in chapter 3. Larger groups are able to lower per unit cost of operations through scale economies; for example, it is less expensive per bomb to plan and execute one hundred, rather than ten, bombings, as fixed costs, which do not vary with the number of bombs, are spread over more bombings. Larger group size also permits enhanced specialization of labor, so that members become more skilled at particular tasks, such as making bombs or casing locations. Bigger groups can also have a political wing that promotes their goals to the public. Enhanced size also allows a group to locate at multiple autonomous bases, which lowers its vulnerability. Larger groups can attract greater resources, particularly in terms of highly skilled members. Thus, Aum Shinrikyo recruited many scientists to develop its biological, chemical, and radiological weapons program (see chapter 7). Greater resources can be used to provide legal counsel. The downside to size is, of course, an increased vulnerability to attack or infiltration, which can be partly managed through multiple locations and loosely tied cells. For the most part, terrorist groups benefit from larger size and are better equipped to achieve a greater presence through a robust campaign and enhanced propaganda.

For governments, size can be both a plus and a minus in their counterterrorism efforts. Size is a plus in bringing resources to bear on such efforts. Larger and more mature governments are more equipped to apply monetary and fiscal policies to cushion the economic impact of terrorist attacks.[20] Larger governments can project power to challenge foreign-based terrorist groups, as the United States has done in Afghanistan, Pakistan, the Philippines, Somalia, and Yemen with special operations and drone strikes. Larger governments possess better intelligence networks and can bring pressures against foreign governments that host terrorist groups.

Government size is, however, a disadvantage when different government agencies either work at cross-purposes or engage in wasteful duplication. Larger governments are plagued by rent-seeking, which are wasteful efforts to gain or maintain control over government resources through competition either among component parts of the government or among outside interests. Agencies will fight to keep an assignment even if a more appropriate agency should take over the task. In other instances, outside contractors will lobby to supply counterterrorism equipment, such as explosive trace portals (ETPs) or "puffer machines" at US airports that were eventually removed from all US airports because of their unreliability.[21] Larger governments are plagued with rent-seeking that affects all aspects of governance, including counterterrorism. In addition, as 9/11 demonstrated, a large government can create communication failures among alternative agencies, so that crucial information is never shared.[22]

Size differences between terrorist groups and their government opponents bring to mind Jack Hirshleifer's "Paradox of Power," which refers to the ability to reach one's goal in the face of opposition.[23] This paradox indicates that a weaker opponent may initially grow stronger relative to its larger adversary. This stems from the underdog exerting more effort and determination than its rival in order to gain a foothold in the face of overwhelming odds. Moreover, the weaker or smaller opponent may possess stealth to strike unseen or by surprise. Small groups may also be more united by the apparently insurmountable odds against them. Often dissent in terrorist groups only develops as they surpass important milestones in terms of their capabilities. This paradox points to two important counterterrorism insights: to strike hard at incipient terrorist groups and not to underestimate small terrorist groups' prowess.

What Is Constituency Asymmetry?

Liberal democracies must maintain support among a majority of voters to win re-election to remain in power. Government officeholders' inability to address terrorist campaigns adequately may cost them their incumbency. Such elected officials may also lose supporters if they respond too harshly to a terrorist threat, thereby compromising democratic principles.

By contrast, terrorist groups can survive with a much smaller constituency, provided that they can fund their operations through extortion, illegal activities, legal activities, or supporters' donations. This relatively smaller constituency puts terrorist groups in a favored position if terrorists seek a specific political change. If, however, the terrorist group intends to overthrow the government, then the terrorists must vie for a constituency nearer in size to, but still smaller than, that of the government.

6

ECONOMIC CONSEQUENCES OF TERRORISM

Why Do Some Terrorist Groups Try to Create Economic Losses?

During the summers of 1985, 1986, and 1987, the Spanish Basque separatist group Euskadi Ta Askatasuna (ETA) carried out a bombing campaign against seaside hotels, visited by European and other tourists. For example, on May 22, 1987, ETA mailed letters warning of a summer bombing campaign to Belgian, British, Swiss, and West German embassies. Prior to each hotel bombing, ETA phoned in warnings in order to minimize casualties. ETA's intention was to hit the profitable Spanish tourist sector as a way of pressuring the Spanish government to concede to ETA's demand for Basque Country independence from Spain.[1] Tourism is an important sector of the Spanish economy that earns foreign exchange. Other European leftist terrorist groups, including the Italian Red Brigades, the Greek 17 November, and the German Red Army Faction (RAF), have targeted business interests as a means of cajoling the government to give into their political demands. This was a favorite tactic of European leftist terrorists, given their anticapitalist orientation and their intention not to cause many casualties.[2]

This anticapitalist orientation is graphically illustrated by the abduction of Hanns Martin Schleyer, the sixty-two-year-old president of the Confederation of German Employers' Associations, on September 5, 1977. Schleyer, who at the time of his kidnapping was West Germany's most famous industrialist, was also the president of the Confederation of Industry and a member of the Mercedes-Benz's board of directors. The daring abduction took place during rush hour in Cologne by ten to fifteen RAF terrorists with automatic rifles, who ambushed Schleyer's two-car convoy as it stopped for an empty baby carriage pushed in front of Schleyer's Mercedes by a female terrorist. The RAF terrorists unleashed a barrage of over two hundred shots at the two-car convoy, killing two police escorts, a bodyguard, and Schleyer's driver. The terrorists then dragged Schleyer unharmed from his car to a waiting minibus and sped away. RAF demanded the release of group members imprisoned in West Germany. The West German authorities did not give into RAF demands; Schleyer was murdered by his captors on October 18, 1977. His kidnapping made West German business executives seek protection, thus leading to a boom in the security services sector.[3] This kidnapping and other assassinations of industrialists sent shockwaves throughout the West German business sector.

A RAND study indicates that the Provisional Irish Republican Army (PIRA) in Northern Ireland targeted key economic interests in its thirty-year campaign for independence as a means of hurting the United Kingdom. This campaign included numerous high-profile bombings in London and throughout England to create economic losses, intended to coerce the British government into granting PIRA's political demands. PIRA's intention to hurt the British economy is vividly illustrated by the Bishopsgate truck bombing on April 24, 1993, in the heart of the London financial district. The bombing resulted in well over a billion dollars in damages and motivated the subsequent widespread use of closed-circuit TV (CCTV) throughout the United Kingdom.[4]

The Tamil Tigers targeted Sri Lankan energy resources and the financial center in Colombo to ratchet up the pressure on the government to concede to its demands for independence. The attacks on 9/11 on the World Trade Center were also aimed at putting stress on the US economy. Apparently, al-Qaeda's online training manual, *Al-Battar*, has often called for attacks on enemy countries' infrastructure and financial assets in order to cause economic losses.[5] Even prior to al-Qaeda's calls, the first attack on the World Trade Center on February 26, 1993, by Ramzi Yousef and accomplices, inspired by Omar Abdel-Rahman (known as the "blind cleric"), was intended to cause significant economic consequences. A massive truck bombing in the underground garage of the North Tower was meant to bring down both towers. The bomb killed six and injured many others, but the towers remained standing despite a massive crater and a half a billion dollars in damages.

There are many additional instances where terrorist groups directed their attacks toward damaging the economy or its infrastructure (for example, utility lines, bridges, or financial markets). The simple answer to the question posed at the outset is that some terrorist groups created economic losses for targeted economies in order to pressure the besieged governments into granting their demands. All terrorism-plagued governments must weigh the benefits against the costs from conceding to terrorists' political demands. Benefits arise from reduced deaths, injuries, property damages, and economic consequences. When, however, these economic ramifications of an ongoing terrorist campaign are made sufficiently large, the targeted government may view the benefits from conceding terrorists' demands as justifying the associated costs. These concessionary costs can involve losing future elections in a democracy or encouraging other terrorist groups to utilize economic tactics to win their demands. That is, there may be a demonstration effect that has the conceding government trade one terror campaign for another.

Throughout this chapter, I delineate the economic consequences of terrorism on the entire economy—the so-called macroeconomic effects—from those on specific firms or sectors—the so-called microeconomic effects. There is no question that a large-scale attack, such as 9/11, can involve significant losses, but in most instances these losses are small with respect to the size of the host economy to the attack. Thus, the impacted economy can typically absorb the loss without displaying much stress. Although terrorists can inflict pain and localized costs on their victims, terrorists have a difficult time in creating adverse consequences for the entire economy of targeted countries. This is particularly true of diversified, advanced industrial economies that can deploy monetary and fiscal policies (defined later in the chapter) to address economic shocks. Moreover, such economies can employ security measures to regain their citizens' sense of safety. One must remember that most countries fortunately experience very few transnational and domestic terrorist events each year and suffer relatively few casualties and little property loss from such attacks. For the United States, the total number of transnational terrorist attacks for 2012–2015 was ten. It was seven for the United Kingdom, nine for France, two for Belgium, and five for Germany.[6] In recent years, the average deaths per incident are about four individuals; hence, there was relatively little loss of life in these countries.

What Are Direct versus Indirect Costs Associated with Terrorist Attacks?

The direct costs of a terrorist event involve the immediate losses associated with the incident and include the value of damaged structures, lives lost, injuries sustained, lost wages, destroyed property, cleanup, and reduced commerce. Any losses imposed on other firms or sectors from the attack are also included. These "spillover costs" may arise from sales losses of suppliers to firms directly damaged by the attack. Economic methods provide alternative means for valuing lives and injuries, including a victim's forgone income stream of earnings, or advanced methods for valuing a "statistical life."

The latter measures the extra pay required to induce someone to accept a riskier means of employment for which the likelihood of death is greater than some comparable employment. Comparable employment means that the education and skill requirements are the same in the two jobs, so that any pay differential can be attributable to the greater risks of death. This method allows for a monetary value to be put on each additional percentage of death and ultimately on the value of living.[7]

Indirect or secondary costs of terrorism concern attack-related subsequent losses, such as higher insurance premiums, augmented security costs, enhanced compensation to those at high-risk locations, and attack-induced long-run changes in commerce. Indirect costs may assume the form of reduced growth in gross domestic product (GDP), losses to foreign direct investment (FDI), changes in inflation, or increases in unemployment. First-responder and recovery measures also entail indirect costs, as do costly behavioral responses to the increased uncertainty following an attack.[8] Some of this behavioral adjustment may include psychological costs of coping with a larger perceived risk of terrorism, stemming from large-scale attacks such as 9/11 or the Madrid commuter train bombing on March 11, 2004 (known as 3/11).

In practice, the distinction between direct and indirect costs requires a judgment that likely differs among analysts. This is why costs estimates concerning an attack, like 9/11, range widely depending on whose analysis one consults, as shown later. Fortunately, this distinction is not really necessary to characterize the annual effect of terrorism, which can be captured by some well-defined macroeconomic aggregate such as lost GDP, reduced GDP per capita growth, or decreased investment. In other instances where a terrorist campaign targets a specific economic sector, a microeconomic measure can better reflect the terrorism-induced losses. Thus, the losses associated with attacks against commercial airlines may correspond to reduced tourist receipts, while attacks leveled against foreign-owned businesses may be represented by reduced FDI in the targeted country. If lost output, casualties, and damaged infrastructure, tied to terrorist attacks, are sufficiently large, then these consequences will affect the economy's productive capacity, with measurable macroeconomic and/or microeconomic ramifications.

At the outset, I must, however, caution that for most countries the incidence and economic consequences of terrorism are thankfully modest. This is because most advanced countries experience very few incidents each year and most attacks are small. Much of the cost of terrorism is embodied in security costs, which actually raise GDP by employing people. Terrorism is not like civil or interstate wars that can leave tens of thousands dead and raze cities, as in the Syrian civil war. Terrorism is more likely to have sector-specific or microeconomic effects.

Do Economic Losses Differ between Domestic and Transnational Terrorist Attacks?

Before addressing this question, I should remind the reader about the differences between the two types of terrorist incidents. Domestic terrorism is homegrown and home-directed; the victims and perpetrators are citizens of the venue country hosting the attack. By contrast, transnational terrorism entangles two or more countries. This international entanglement stems from the nationalities of the victims or perpetrators in relation to the venue country. For instance, 3/11 was a transnational terrorist event because the 192 people killed included citizens from seventeen countries other than Spain. Moreover, the perpetrators included some Moroccan citizens.[9]

Domestic terrorist incidents far outnumber transnational terrorist incidents, as shown in chapter 1. Moreover, domestic terrorism tends to be associated with civil wars and ethnonationalist conflicts, while transnational terrorism may, but need not, be associated with interstate wars. Given its ability to affect more than one country, a *single transnational terrorist attack* generally has more adverse influence on the venue country's economy than a single domestic terrorist attack.[10] This follows because the international implications of transnational terrorist attacks have the potential of affecting trade, FDI, and tourism as perceived risks increase. But the *overall* effect of domestic terrorism may be greater than that of transnational terrorism because a country generally sustains far more domestic than transnational terrorist incidents.

How Much Did 9/11 Cost in Terms of Economic Losses?

This is a surprisingly difficult question to answer because researchers include widely different costs in their estimates of the direct and indirect costs of 9/11. Some researchers include the costs of the US-led Afghanistan War in the costs of 9/11. This practice makes the costs of 9/11 astronomically high. This is also true of including the costs of the US-led Iraq War, started on March 20, 2003. Other researchers add the large increase in defensive expenditures embodied in the Department of Homeland Security (DHS) budget to the indirect costs of 9/11. None of these costs seem appropriate. Protection of the US homeland did not necessarily require the Afghanistan invasion. In the case of the Iraq War, there was no evidence uncovered that Iraq harbored terrorists at the time of the invasion. After the invasion and the instability that followed, Iraq became the home of al-Qaeda in Iraq, which eventually morphed into Islamic State in Iraq and Syria (ISIS). Furthermore, some increases in the homeland security expenditure were warranted as the vulnerabilities uncovered by 9/11 showed. That is, homeland security was underfunded before 9/11 and needed to be increased even without 9/11.

More sensible cost estimates try to gauge the immediate people and property losses of 9/11 along with cleanup, economic disruption, and recovery costs. This more reasonable cost estimate is $80–$90 billion during a time when the

US GDP was $10.6 trillion. Thus, 9/11, the biggest terrorist event in modern history, accounted for about 0.008 percent of US GDP.[11] These costs can be broken down into direct costs of $48.7 billion and indirect costs of about $31–$41 billion. The Bureau of Economic Analysis (BEA) put the damage to structures and equipment (including the destruction of the World Trade Center) at $16.2 billion. The private sector lost about $3.3 billion from work disruption, layoffs, and a two-day partial work stoppage. This loss is partly offset by $0.8 billion in wage gains for state and local government workers, such as police and firefighters. Another large direct cost was the loss in human lives, whose value was between $8 and $20 billion depending on the value placed on a human life.[12]

One may ask how the $80–$90 billion costs of 9/11 compare with the smaller 3/11 Madrid commuter train bombing. Direct costs of 3/11 amounted to $335 million, which was 0.03 percent of Spain's GDP at the time.[13] Indirect costs for 3/11 have not been estimated. Actually, the direct costs of 3/11 accounted for a much larger percentage of Spain's GDP than the approximately 0.005 percent of US GDP for the direct costs of 9/11. The direct losses from both 9/11 and 3/11 still amounted to a relatively small portion of GDP, which most advanced industrial economies can withstand with little stress, especially if assisted by government policies.

How Did the US Government's Policies Cushion the Impact of 9/11?

Monetary policy is achieved as the country's central bank adjusts interest rates and the availability of funds. The interest rate is the cost of borrowing. If this cost is brought down by monetary policy during a severe terrorist attack, then affected individuals can borrow money to replace lost assets, thereby cushioning the economic disruption in spending stemming from the terrorist attack. Moreover, lower interest rates encourage investment, which may offset some reduced economic activity associated with the uncertainty from the large-scale terrorist attack. Action by the central bank to lower borrowing costs is known as expansionary monetary policy. To offset economic losses tied to a terrorist attack, the central bank can also increase available funds in the banking system, which results in an increase in *liquidity*. Fiscal policy is action by the government to affect taxes or government spending. Decreases in taxes denote expansionary fiscal policy, as do increases in government spending. To offset the negative economic consequences of a large-sale terrorist attack, expansionary fiscal policy is appropriate.

Prior to 9/11, the US economy was slipping into recession. Throughout 2000, US GDP was flat; during the first two quarters of 2001, GDP was falling owing to the recession. This recession is consistent with consumer confidence falling precipitously prior to 9/11 and the unemployment rate rising before and immediately after 9/11. In fact, the demand for air travel was way down, as reflected by the relatively few passengers on all four of the wide-body hijacked flights on 9/11.[14]

Immediately following 9/11, financial markets were in disarray as bond market trading was suspended for a day and stock market trading was suspended until the week following 9/11. When times are uncertain as they were after the four hijackings, asset holders increase their portfolios' share of highly liquid assets. To accommodate this surging demand for liquidity, the US Federal Reserve System sharply cut key interest rates, thereby making funds available for investment and precautionary holding of liquid assets. This monetary policy assuaged any possible liquidity concerns or runs on banks for cash. Fiscal policy also performed a supportive role. Fortuitously, a major tax cut had been signed into law in May 2001, five months prior to 9/11. Since such tax cuts take almost six months before impacting the economy, the required stimulus came just when needed after the hijackings and their consequences. This tax-cut expansionary effect was bolstered by an increase of a $40 billion supplemental appropriation for emergency spending that had been approved by the US Congress after 9/11. This spending was earmarked for search-and-rescue efforts at the four crash sites and tightening security at US airports and other vulnerable venues. In addition to the needed disaster relief, this government spending surge gave a powerful stimulus to aggregate expenditure. Remember that this increased spending was almost exactly that of the direct cost of 9/11. Moreover, increased military spending, associated with the US-led invasion of Afghanistan, provided a stimulant to aggregate US spending. As a consequence, the US budget deficit grew.

These monetary and fiscal policies bolstered the post-9/11 US economy as real disposable income (the after-tax income of households) grew sharply by the first quarter of 2002. US consumption of durables (for example, cars and appliances) jumped right after 9/11, fueled by lower interest rates and the tax cut. President Bush had appealed to patriotism and asked people to purchase large-ticket items to support the economy. Real GDP started a sustained upward recovery trend beginning in the last quarter of 2001. This increase was accompanied by a rise in industrial production at the start of 2002. Although the US economy recovered immediately following 9/11, unemployment did not fall until the last half of 2002. Unemployment usually recovers with a lag following any economic downturn. All in all, al-Qaeda did not succeed in hurting the US economy as intended with the attacks on 9/11. In fact, some may argue that these attacks set in motion fiscal and monetary policies that reversed the ensuing recession that had begun before the four hijackings.

One major consideration that keeps developed economies resilient to major terrorist attacks is their well-functioning monetary and fiscal policies that can limit any terrorism-induced adverse economic impact. Less-developed countries are more likely to be less resilient to large-scale attacks because their fiscal and monetary policies are less likely to be carried out so quickly and effectively. Again, I must reiterate that the US tax cut coming in May 2001 was just good fortune with respect to the rapid post-9/11 recovery. Since most terrorist attacks cause relatively little loss of life and property, fiscal and monetary policies are not required for most terrorist attacks.

Do Terrorist Attacks Affect Stock Markets?

Major conflicts have affected the value of stock exchanges. For instance, the sinking of the *Lusitania* on May 7, 1915, dropped the Dow Jones Industrial Average (DJIA) stock values by over 5 percent on the day following the sinking and by 16 percent on the sixth day after the sinking. It took twenty-one days for DJIA stock values to regain their presinking average values. For the German invasion of France on May 12, 1940, it took 795 days for DJIA stock values to rebound; for the Pearl Harbor attack on December 7, 1941, it took 232 days for DJIA stock values to rebound. After the August 2, 1990, Iraq invasion of Kuwait, the DJIA stock values rebounded in 134 days.[15]

With the exception of 9/11, major terrorist attacks have not negatively influenced overall stock exchange values or returns for more than a matter of days. For example, the following large-scale terrorist attacks and their effect on DJIA stock exchange averages are noted: the US Marines barracks bombing in Beirut on October 23, 1983, depressed stock values for one day; the downing of Air India Boeing 747 on June 21, 1985, lowered stock values for four days; the downing of Pan Am Flight 103 on December 21, 1988, reduced stock values for three days; the World Trade Center truck bombing on February 26, 1993, adversely affected stock values for one day; the bombing of the Alfred P. Murrah Federal Building in Oklahoma City on April 19, 1995, depressed stock values for one day; and the US embassies bombings in Kenya and Tanzania on August 7, 1998, lowered stock values for one day.

The notable exception is 9/11, when stock values fell by almost 11 percent within six days of the attack, wiping out trillions of dollars of capitalized value. However, the world stock markets displayed an amazing resilience. Within twenty trading days, six of thirty-three stock exchanges had recovered their pre-9/11 stock values; within forty trading days, twenty-one had recouped their pre-9/11 stock values. Two months after 9/11, twenty-seven stock exchanges had returned to their pre-9/11 average values.[16] Thus, 9/11 did have an adverse, but rather temporary, impact on global stock exchanges. But one must remember that 9/11 was like no other previous terrorist attack. Furthermore, 9/11 came at a time when recession was looming for many major industrial countries, thereby adding to the fragility of world stock exchanges.

Future terrorist incidents must exceed the carnage or the destruction of 9/11 to have a similar impact on world stock exchanges, which are now more resilient because of the experience with 9/11. A dirty bomb that disperses radiological material in a major city, such as Los Angeles or New York City, could easily have a greater effect on world stock exchanges than 9/11 even though the dirty bomb kills few people. The bomb's adverse effect comes from closing down a major commerce venue, such as the Los Angeles port, during the extended cleanup period.[17]

The stock prices of specific impacted sectors can display much longer-term adverse consequences from a large-scale terrorist incident. This was the case for airline stocks after 9/11. On average, the major world airline stocks took eighty-four trading days to recover their pre-9/11 stock values.[18] Other travel-related firms and hotels were greatly affected by 9/11.

Finally, countries plagued by an ongoing terrorist campaign have displayed greater negative impacts of terrorist attacks on their stock markets. This was the case for Israel during 1990–2003 when 1,212 Israelis were killed and another 5,726 injured in terrorist attacks.[19] Large-scale suicide terrorist attacks had the greatest longer-term adverse effect on Israeli stock exchanges. Nevertheless, Israeli and world stock exchanges have shown resilience to terrorist campaigns.

What Are the Main Macroeconomic Consequences of Terrorist Attacks?

After 9/11, economists quantified the impact of transnational terrorist attacks on the growth of GDP per capita (that is, national income per person) in countries experiencing such attacks. In one influential study, each year that a country experienced transnational terrorist attacks resulted in a mere 0.048 percent fall in GDP per capita growth.[20] This is a rather small decline given that countries grow at an average GDP per capita rate of 2.0 percent. Thus, terrorists have not had their intended influence on targeted countries' growth. Some studies find an even smaller negative effect on GDP per capita growth. In all studies, the negative influences of transnational terrorism on GDP per capita growth are always very modest.[21]

Based on past research, I can draw some conclusions with respect to the macroeconomic consequences of terrorism. First, studies involving many countries at either the global or regional level find a very small terrorism-induced reduction in GDP per capita growth, consumption, or GDP. Second, any reduction in GDP per capita growth is traced to increased government expenditure or decreased investment. Government spending increases are tied to enhanced counterterrorism measures, while investment decreases as public investment in counterterrorism crowds out or limits funds for private investment. Counterterrorism spending is often less growth-promoting than government spending on infrastructure, education, fostering innovations, or social welfare. Third, transnational terrorist attacks are more harmful than an equivalent number of domestic terrorist attacks on economic growth. Fourth, civil wars have a much larger negative influence on economic growth than any form of terrorism. Fifth, developing countries are more apt than developed countries to have their economic growth reduced by terrorism.

A recent study revisits the debate over terrorism and economic growth. In so doing, this new study accounts for biases that arise from interdependency among countries' terrorist attacks. These biases are predicted to overstate the harmful effect of terrorism on economic growth. When these biases are eliminated, the new study finds *no adverse effect of terrorism on economic growth for an average country*.[22] This is really good news for us and really bad news for terrorists bent on harming economies. Since most developed countries experience very few terrorist attacks each year, this new finding is believable. It is even more credible because these countries lose few lives and little property annually from terrorist attacks. Even recent terrorist attacks in England and other European countries resulted in relatively little loss of lives and property when compared to the size of the overall economy or the population.

What Types of Targeted Countries Are Most Affected Economically by Terrorism?

If the average country can withstand terrorist attacks with little macroeconomic consequence, then what targeted countries' economies are affected by terrorism? The answer is easy. A large terrorist campaign in a small country is sure to have measurable implications for economic growth and GDP. In the case of Israel, the economic consequences of the Second Intifada during 2000–2003 translated into a loss of about 10 percent of Israel's GDP. This Palestinian uprising lasted into 2005. There was a similar loss in GDP for the Basque Country during the ETA terrorist campaign for independence over a twenty-year period. In fact, terrorist campaigns in small countries affect consumption, investment, and exports.[23] Thus, the message is simple. Small, terrorism-plagued countries are negatively impacted by terrorist campaigns, unlike most countries that experience little terrorism annually or are sufficiently large and diversified to absorb the few terrorist attacks with little, if any, economic effects.

These small terrorism-challenged countries are disadvantaged in many ways. First, they generally possess few resources to mount an effective proactive campaign to annihilate the terrorists. This is particularly true if the terrorists are based in a neighboring country. Second, these small countries are often not so diversified that one sector or province can compensate for losses incurred in other sectors or provinces. Third, these small countries may lack sufficient defensive resources to shore up vulnerable infrastructure or border crossings. Fourth, even small losses may loom large in a small economy. Fifth, many small, less-advanced countries cannot practice sophisticated monetary and fiscal policies to cushion the adverse effects of a terrorist campaign. Sixth, some small countries are institutionally challenged in terms of the rule of law and governance.[24]

An apt small-country example is Yemen, which sustained two major attacks on its ports within a two-year period. On October 12, 2000, the USS *Cole* was rammed by a small motorboat, laden with a large bomb (see chapter 5). Less than two years later, on October 6, 2002, al-Qaeda terrorists in a small motorboat blew a twenty-six-foot-wide hole in the French supertanker *Limburg* when it was five miles off of the coast of Yemen. At the time of the attack, the *Limburg* was waiting to be tugged into the Yemeni port of Mina al-Dabah.[25] These two terrorist attacks greatly harmed Yemen's shipping industry; half of its port activities were diverted to competitive facilities in Djibouti and Oman due to a tripling of insurance premiums for Yemen's ports.[26] This diversion resulted in a loss of $3.8 million per month to the country's shipping industry, which amounted to half of Yemen's shipping revenues at the time. Such losses are huge for a country like Yemen, which is heavily dependent on a few sectors. Yemen's port operations contribute significantly to the country's GDP, given its ideal location at the juncture of the Red Sea and the Arabian Sea. To win back the port activity, Yemen needed to make a costly investment in security.

What Are the Microeconomic Sectoral Consequences of Terrorism?

Even though most advanced economies sustain little macroeconomic consequences from their terrorist attacks, this may not be the case at a microeconomic sectoral level, especially if an attack targets a specific industrial sector. For instance, terrorist attacks directed at tourist venues (for example, airports, hotels, and public attractions) may make tourists reconsider their planned vacations. If terrorists favor one Mediterranean country over another, then a tourist may be expected to visit the less-risky country, particularly if other amenities in the two countries are equivalent. A pioneering study on tourism and terrorism shows that every transnational terrorist attack in Spain during 1970–1991 dissuaded 140,000 tourists from visiting Spain.[27] This translates into a sizable amount of lost tourist revenue when the reduced number of tourists is multiplied by the average spending per tourist. A follow-up study examines the effects of transnational terrorist attacks on the lucrative tourist industry in Austria, France, Greece, and Italy during 1974–1988, when these countries sustained some high-profile terrorist attacks on airports and other tourist-sensitive venues. For Greece, the cumulated sum of all tourism revenue losses amounted to 23.4 percent of the country's annual tourism revenue for 1988, while for Austria, the cumulated sum of all tourism revenue losses amounted to 40.7 percent of the country's annual tourism revenue for 1988. Austria was particularly hard hit by terrorist attacks directed against Jewish interests during 1979–1980 and the infamous Abu Nidal Organization's attack on the Vienna airport on December 27, 1985. By contrast, Italy lost only the equivalent of 6 percent of its 1988 tourism revenues from its terrorist attacks. Despite numerous terrorist attacks, France did not display a significant loss of its 1988 tourism revenues. Apparently, larger economies are better able to withstand tourism-related terrorist attacks without suffering tourism losses.[28]

A subsequent study investigates the adverse effects of transnational terrorism on tourism for Greece, Israel, and Turkey for 1991–2000. In this study, terrorism cost Greece 9 percent of its tourism market share. Turkey lost just over 5 percent of its tourism market share, while Israel lost less than 1 percent of its tourism market share. Nearly 89 percent of lost tourism due to terrorism in Europe flowed to safer tourist venues in other countries.[29] After many waves of terrorism, researchers calculate the effect of terrorism on tourism in the impacted country. Typically, a measurable consequence is uncovered for small countries experiencing a number of terrorist incidents or a large-scale incident.[30] However, these losses generally end shortly after the attacks stop and the airlines discount fares to entice passengers back. Tourism-dependent countries limit the duration of their terrorism-induced tourism losses through aggressive advertising campaigns touting the country's beauty and attraction. Studies show that potential tourists have a short memory with respect to terrorism; their memory can be made even shorter through fare savings and enticing advertising! In addition, countries augment security at previously vulnerable venues to allay tourists' safety concerns.

Tourists may generalize from Islamic extremists' attacks leveled against Western citizens. That is, tourists from the victims' country may avoid all Muslim countries, even those not involved in the original attack. Moreover, tourists from other Western countries may avoid travel to the Islamic country that was the site of the original attack. Western tourists may generalize still further and avoid travel to all Islamic countries. Thus, a terrorist attack can have negative consequences or spillovers in other destination and origin countries.[31] Such spillovers can make tourism losses larger than generally presupposed in past studies.

Another sector of the economy that is particularly vulnerable to transnational terrorism is FDI, which consists of foreign-owned and foreign-controlled investment in a host country. Terrorists may target FDI as a way of lashing out at a foreign country for which they harbor grievances. This is true of 17 November attacks against US FDI in Greece and ETA attacks against French FDI in Spain. Terrorist risk raises the cost of doing business, as expensive security measures must be deployed and personnel must be duly compensated and protected. FDI attacks also increase insurance premiums. As these expenses rise owing to FDI-directed attacks, investors can be anticipated to redirect their investments to safer countries. This redirection takes time, as FDI holdings must be sold. An initial study shows that transnational terrorism lowered net annual FDI in Spain by 13.5 percent and in Greece by 11.9 percent. These are sizable losses for two small economies that are heavily dependent on FDI as a source of savings to support growth and the host country's own investment.[32]

There are many recent studies of the impact of terrorism on FDI. Terrorism has a greater detrimental influence on FDI in developing countries than in developed countries. This finding carries on the theme that developed countries can better insulate themselves from the economic backlash of terrorism. Nevertheless, a heightened terrorism risk reduces FDI to some extent even in developed countries, as such attacks increase uncertainty, which harms investment. Even US FDI is adversely affected when terrorist incidents abroad target US interests and investment holdings. Generally, transnational terrorism risk is more damaging than domestic terrorism risk for FDI.[33]

Researchers also establish a negative relationship between trade and terrorist attacks in either trading partner. A doubling of the number of terrorist incidents is found to reduce bilateral trade by 4 percent, so that high-terrorism countries may suffer a substantial reduction in their trade volume. Trade falls for the same reasons that terrorism reduces FDI; namely, terrorism raises the costs of doing business. This follows because terrorism raises uncertainty, insurance costs, wage premiums, and security expenditures. Increased security at ports of entry and exit can slow the transit of goods and act like a tax or tariff.

Transnational terrorism is seen to imply a larger negative impact than domestic terrorism on trade flows between trading partners. In addition, terrorism has a smaller negative effect on trade than other forms of conflict, such as civil wars, coups, interstate wars, or guerrilla wars. This agrees with terrorism being a less damaging form of political violence than these alternatives. Terrorism has a greater effect on manufactured-than on primary-goods trade. Presumably, alternative supply sources for primary goods are more limited than for manufactured goods, so that a country may have to stay with its supplier of some primary goods despite the terrorism risk.[34]

What Are Some General Principles Regarding the Economic Impact of Terrorism?

There are many guiding principles with respect to the economic impact of terrorism.[35] For most economies, the macroeconomic consequences of terrorism are rather modest and of a short-term nature. Advanced economies possess automatic stabilizers (for example, unemployment insurance) that offset short-term employment losses in the case of a large-scale terrorist attack or a terrorist campaign. These automatic stabilizers are bolstered by discretionary monetary and fiscal policies that lower interest rates, augment liquidity, or raise government expenditures to adjust to short-term shocks following from significant terrorist attacks. Large diversified economies are able to withstand terrorism and curb economic losses as economic activities shift away from terrorism-impacted sectors to less-impacted sectors. This transfer of activities is also true regionally. During the height of the ETA terrorist campaign, economic activities moved from the Basque Country to more tranquil Spanish provinces. One must remember that cleanup and recovery efforts following large-scale terrorist incidents create short-term employment that partly offset employment losses associated with large-scale attacks. In the longer term, terrorist campaigns result in new jobs in law enforcement, homeland security, and intelligence. Jobs are also associated with the rebuilding of destroyed property. These new employment opportunities also act as an automatic stabilizer. Well-developed institutions cushion the consequences of terrorism.

Small countries, plagued with significant terrorist campaigns, display worrisome macroeconomic consequences in terms of losses in consumption, investment, GDP, and economic growth. This is particularly true of some developing countries that possess poor monetary and fiscal institutions. Most failed states have weak institutions to offset macroeconomic costs stemming from terrorist attacks. These states are particularly challenged because they cannot exercise control throughout the country, so that resident terrorist groups can operate with impunity. It is these small, institutionally challenged countries wherein terrorist campaigns can extract a significant toll in many ways. For example, more educated citizens will migrate to seek sanctuaries in safer countries.[36] Investments will leave the country for less-risky and higher returns abroad. Trade will also decline owing to terrorism risk. As the small country loses GDP, there are fewer resources for the government to use to mount an effective counterterrorism offensive. Essentially, the deck is stacked against small failed states.

At the microeconomic level, the most vulnerable sectors are tourism, FDI, and exports. The immediate costs of most terrorist attacks are localized, thereby causing a substitution of economic activity away from a vulnerable sector to relatively safer sectors. Changes in prices, wages, and interest rates can redirect raw materials, labor, and capital quickly in the face of terrorism-induced risk. More advanced and larger economies are more adept at performing this stabilizing process, thereby limiting the ability of terrorists, even at the sectoral level, to create much economic hardship for very long. Again, developing countries are less skilled at this automatic-stabilizing process and, in turn, experience more economic stress at the sectoral level from terrorism. However, even when losses occur at the sectoral level, these economic consequences are small compared to the affected country's overall GDP.

The bottom line is that most economies can weather the average amount of terrorism with few or no economic consequences. Countries must be either plagued with terrorism or else possess poorly developed institutions to suffer much terrorism-induced economic loss. Even in the case of the former, countries, for example, Israel, rebound quickly after the intensity of the terrorism abates.

7

THE FUTURE OF TERRORISM

How Are Forecasts about Terrorism Made?

As long as there are grievances, there will be conflict and, thus, terrorism. Since the start of recorded history, terrorism has played a role in politics and will continue to do so. Terrorism provides a cost-effective means for a subnational group to gain a presence through extortion-based violence or its threat. For example, a relatively cheap truck bomb can cause over a billion dollars of damage, as in the Bishopsgate bombing on April 24, 1993, in the heart of London's financial district. The Provisional Irish Republican Army (PIRA) was responsible for this high-profile bombing on the British mainland to create maximum cost. More recently, an ISIS-inspired truck-ramming attack along the waterfront of Nice, France, on July 14, 2016, killed eighty-six pedestrians and injured hundreds of others. This inexpensive attack captured headlines around the world for weeks and inspired similar kinds of attacks that continue to this day in other countries. Such attacks allow terrorist groups to grab the attention of the public and the government.

Since the start of the modern era of terrorism in the late 1960s, terrorist experts have wanted to predict future terrorism trends based on recent experiences or statistical depictions of terrorist attacks. Two forecasting paradigms are common. The first uses the nature of recent attacks and the identity of the perpetrators to predict future attacks.[1] For example, a spate of suicide attacks by religious fundamentalist terrorists are predicted to continue into the foreseeable future. This is a reactive prediction method that is no more sophisticated than a naive weather-forecasting model that predicts that tomorrow's weather will be the same as today's weather. Such weather predictions are right about two-thirds of the time. In the case of terrorism, this naive prediction model fails miserably because new behavioral drivers are constantly and unexpectedly surfacing with new grievances, new groups, and attack innovations. For instance, past predictions of leftist-directed terrorist attacks with relatively few casualties were adequate in the 1970s until the rise of state-sponsored terrorism in the 1980s and the emerging dominance of religious-based terrorism in the late 1990s. The transition to more state-sponsored attacks resulted in more carnage and collateral damage. Moreover, the transition from fewer leftist and more religious-based terrorist attacks meant that suicide bombings became more prevalent. As a consequence of these unforeseen transitions, past predictions of casualties per terrorist attack lost their validity (see chapter 1 on how casualties per attack changed over time). The one certainty is that new drivers will always arise, and, as they do, past experience-based predictions become less accurate or obsolete. Today, many experts view the use of trucks and cars to plow down pedestrians as the new normal because of incidences in Nice, Stockholm, Berlin, London, New York, and elsewhere. This recent incident-driven prediction will change quickly once the next inexpensive attack innovation surfaces. Really useful predictions are able to guess this innovation, but this cannot be done by forecasting from recently observed attacks.

The second paradigm of forecasting is based on statistical methods, where forecasts are made by extrapolating the current pattern in the data for some postdata years. That is, the researcher relies upon the observed data points—say, skyjackings per month—to estimate a temporal pattern for attacks that may include trends, cycles, or other characteristics. Once the statistical representation is built and tested, the representation is then employed to forecast the number of attacks outside of the range of the data.[2] If the data is for 1968–2015, then the estimated relationship is utilized to forecast the number of attacks for 2016 and some years beyond. If, for example, kidnappings are estimated to have been growing at 5 percent, one could forecast a 5 percent growth into the foreseeable future. Further suppose that skyjackings follow a four-year cyclical pattern; then a peak in skyjackings should be followed by a downturn, and a trough (or low level of attacks) should be followed by an upturn. Such forecasts based on statistical techniques become less accurate as they are projected further beyond the observed data points. Just like experience-based predictions, a statistically fitted forecast cannot foresee shocks or changes in behavioral patterns. Quite simply, forecasts offer an "average" picture of the past that cannot capture unanticipated innovations.

Although I am not a big fan of forecasting based on observing a few noteworthy incidents—the so-called experience-based forecasting paradigm, I do see value in statistical-based forecasting even though its accuracy wanes when predicting further into the future. The latter cautions us not to predict more than two or three years into the future and to update the forecasting model when new data become available. As the model's underlying data are updated, the representative forecasting model starts to incorporate data-embodied innovations. To illustrate, I will relate a relevant personal experience. In 2000, I coauthored an article that made the audacious prediction that terrorism was becoming "more threatening," with some high-carnage terrorist attacks anticipated.[3] Our data-driven forecasting model reflected the rising severity of religious fundamentalist terrorist attacks. Before the article was accepted and published, one reviewer asked us to remove "becoming more threatening" from the article's title, because it would make readers unduly concerned that a big terrorist attack was imminent. We refused the reviewer's request and kindly asked the journal's editor to permit our title and its implicit warning. He granted our request and the article's title remained unchanged.[4] After 9/11, journalists' google searches pointed to our article as portending a big terrorist attack and greater concerns about rising carnage. We did not predict 9/11; rather, we discerned a larger prevalence of high-casualty terrorist attacks based on a statistical representation of decades of attacks.

Could Forecasts Have Been Used to Predict 9/11?

After 9/11, a public debate ensued involving Richard Clarke (the head of US counterterrorism during 9/11), George Tenet (the CIA director during 9/11), and the White House as to whether 9/11 could have been predicted beforehand and stopped. Clarke and Tenet held that greater attention to details and better sharing of information among US government agencies would have alerted officials to the pending 9/11 attacks. A contrary position was taken by Secretary of State Colin Powell and National Security Adviser Condoleezza Rice.[5]

In February 1998, Osama bin Laden had issued a fatwa against the United States for its having "declared war against God."[6] Bin Laden and the other signatories of the fatwa called on every Muslim to murder Americans anywhere on earth. In a subsequent interview with ABC television, Osama bin Laden stated, "We believe that the worst thieves in the world today and the worst terrorists are the Americans. Nothing could stop you except perhaps retaliation in kind. We do not have to differentiate between military and civilian." This fatwa against America and the pre-9/11 al-Qaeda-directed terrorist attacks, such as the simultaneous bombing of the US embassies in Kenya and Tanzania on August 7, 1998, and the bombing of the USS Cole on October 12, 2000, clearly indicated al-Qaeda's intention to carry out the fatwa. However, it is a far cry from this realization and predicting 9/11.

Let me take a different approach to predicting 9/11 that is somewhat more in keeping with the National Counterterrorism Center (NCTC) that evolved in 2004 from the Terrorist Threat Integration Center. The NCTC collects a large database on terrorism in order to discern patterns and foresee large-scale attacks. This latter task is based on building sophisticated statistical models. The NCTC also collects big data on phone calls and other communications that could prove valuable if there is credible evidence that a terrorist attack is being planned.

I only want to consider the efficacy of building sophisticated forecasting models to identify the "next" 9/11. To do so, coauthors and I applied a host of state-of-the-art statistical forecasting tools to pre-9/11 terrorism data in order to identify any breaks or aberration in the data that could have hinted at 9/11. In fact, the only aberration that we uncovered was a pronounced *downturn in terrorist attacks and skyjackings* in particular after 1999 and the declaration of the fatwa. This is opposite to what we had expected. After an exhaustive statistical analysis, we concluded that sophisticated statistical-based analysis would not have predicted 9/11. We strongly doubt that any such statistical analysis can foresee a particular coming terrorist incident, no matter how large.[7]

Why Is Human Intelligence on Terrorism So Essential?

Given the limited possibilities of statistical modeling to predict the next big terrorist incident, the authorities must rely on human intelligence to "connect the dots" and stop future terrorist attacks. An apt example is the British government's arrest in August 2006 of two dozen alleged al-Qaeda-inspired individuals who were planning to blow up as many as ten transatlantic commercial flights with improvised liquid bombs. Targeted carriers included American, Continental, United, and British Airways. The arrests eventually resulted in the conviction of some of those apprehended for conspiracy to murder. Others of those arrested were not convicted and still others did not stand trial. Apparently, the investigation began in 2005 when a Muslim informant went to the British authorities about a suspicious acquaintance. This tip led to a long investigation and an arrest prior to the planned plot being executed.[8] This uncovered plot led to the restriction of liquids in carry-on luggage.

During 2017, acting on intelligence about an alleged ISIS plot to use laptops and iPads as bombs, the US government banned large electronic devices from the cabins of passenger flights originating from many Middle Eastern airports. This ban was later softened for some Middle East–based airlines that developed better screening procedures for electronic devices. Once again, the usefulness of human intelligence in averting disasters in air is seen. This plot was initially uncovered when US intelligence learned that ISIS had been testing the passage of laptop-rigged bombs through airport screening devices, seized from airports in ISIS-overrun cities.

Since 9/11, there have been many terrorist acts that have been stopped at the planning stage owing to human intelligence. When there is reasonable suspicion of a pending terrorist attack, NCTC big data on phone calls and other forms of communications can be useful in pursuing a credible tip. There must, however, be clear judicial oversight so that big data are not used as an invasion of privacy. All forms of surveillance imply a civil liberty versus safety trade-off that is very difficult to address.

What Is Cyberterrorism and Does It Pose a Future Threat?

Cyberterrorism is the politically motivated use of computer networks, data, and software by subnational groups to threaten or cause violence to noncombatants in order to intimidate a wider audience. In contrast, cyberwar consists of sovereign states using cyberspace in a malicious manner against other states. The unleashing of a computer virus on Iran's nuclear facilities is an example of cyberwarfare. In this book, I am only interested in cyberterrorism involving subnational actors.

Although cyberterrorist attacks have appeared in countless television shows and movies and *are* a possibility, I am aware of no cyberterrorist attack that resulted in death or injury thus far. Two cybersecurity and cyberwar experts write the following about cyberterrorism: "Thirty-one thousand three hundred. That's roughly the number of magazine and journal articles so far that discuss the phenomenon of cyberterrorism. Zero. That's the number of people who had been physically hurt or killed by cyberterrorism."[9] This is not to say that terrorists would not exploit cyberspace to wreak death and destruction if they could gain the expertise. Apparently, computers found in al-Qaeda caves in Afghanistan in 2001 showed the group's interest in causing a dam failure through the use of hacked software.[10] There are surely other wishful plots of terrorists to hack into infrastructure (for example, trains, air-traffic control systems, and nuclear power plants) in order to cause deaths, injuries, and destruction. Fortunately, such efforts require computer skills, inside information, and engineering knowledge that terrorist groups have not yet assembled. Terrorists must do more than gain entry to the system to cause violence. If such an attack were to ever occur, it would likely be perpetrated by religious fundamentalist terrorists, who are prepared to kill indiscriminately. Given so many other, less-demanding means for causing violence, I do not view cyberterrorism to be very likely in the near future, except on a very small scale—say, hacking someone's defibrillator in an assassination attempt.

Cyberterrorism is different from using the Internet to extort a ransom. The planting and use of ransomware is a criminal act that is not motivated for political purposes. When ransomware is used against a hospital, patients' postponed surgeries could result in deaths, but this does not truly fit the definition of cyberterrorism. If, however, a terrorist group used ransomware to gain funds to finance its operations in the pursuit of a political agenda, then this would constitute cyberterrorism if some lives were threatened. I view terrorists' use of ransom-ware as unlikely because they possess much easier ways of extorting money through kidnappings.

As mentioned throughout this book, terrorists exploit cyberspace to facilitate their operations. When ISIS terrorists post videos of beheadings or the murder of a captured Jordanian pilot, the Internet is used not only to get their message across, but also to recruit members. Nevertheless, this use of cyberspace is not cyberterrorism per se insofar as the application of cyberspace is not directly creating violence. Terrorist groups rely on the Internet for communicating, gathering information, sharing innovations (for example, tactics and procedures), and spreading propaganda. In so doing, the Internet facilitates their terrorist campaign. By using the Internet, terrorist groups become vulnerable to Internet-based counterterrorism actions that, among other things, may allow members to be tracked through their communications. However, new apps that encrypt communication hamper such tracking. Also, the authorities can utilize cyberspace to educate the public and to refute terrorist propaganda. Governments can deploy worms and malware to compromise terrorist websites. In other cases, the authorities can replace content on terrorist websites—for example, British intelligence replaced some how-to content in al-Qaeda in the Arabian Peninsula's (AQAP) *Inspire* magazine with a cupcake recipe.[11] Thus, the Internet may both assist and hamper terrorist groups as the terrorists and the authorities match wits.

Will Terrorist Attacks Remain Mostly Low Tech?

Low-tech terrorist attacks rely on bombs and guns. Such attacks require relatively little training or expertise, so they are inexpensive and can cause an unfortunate amount of death and damage. Bombs smuggled onto commercial flights have caused mass casualties, as was true of the downing of an Air India Boeing 747 en route from Montreal to London on June 23,

1985. Sikh extremists were responsible for the deaths of 329 people on board, the fifth deadliest plane crash on record. Other mass-casualty airplane downings include the downing of Pan Am Flight 103 over Lockerbie, Scotland, on December 21, 1988 (270 deaths) and the downing of Union des Transport Aériens (UTA) Flight 772 over Chad on September 19, 1989 (171 deaths).

Large casualty counts have also been associated with low-tech terrorist bombings—for instance, the suicide truck bombing of the US Marines barracks in Beirut on October 23, 1983 (241 deaths); thirteen bombings in Bombay on March 12, 1993 (317 deaths); simultaneous bombings of the US embassies in Nairobi, Kenya, and Dar es Salaam, Tanzania, on August 7, 1998 (301 deaths); the four hijackings on 9/11 (almost 3,000 deaths); bombings of commuter trains and stations in Madrid on March 11, 2004 (191 deaths); and the barricade and hostage seizure of schoolchildren and parents at the Beslan middle school on September 1, 2004 (385 deaths).[12] These incidents are only representative large-carnage terrorist attacks. Low-tech truck ramming of pedestrians have resulted in large carnage— the Nice, France, truck ramming on July 14, 2016, killed eighty-six and injured over four hundred people.

There are a number of reasons why low-tech attacks will remain the most prevalent kind of terrorist attack by far. First, low-tech attacks can kill at relatively low cost; there is literally more bang for the buck compared to high-tech attacks. This is particularly true of suicide attacks. Second, low-tech attacks require few operatives and can be performed by loosely knit cells. As many terrorist groups loosen and cut ties among members to limit vulnerability, these groups must rely on low-tech attacks.[13] Third, as I will show later, low-tech terrorist attacks put terrorist groups at lower risk than most high-tech attacks. For example, dirty bombs and chemical attacks pose a handling risk to the terrorists. Fourth, low-tech attacks are particularly suited to lone wolf terrorists, who must be self-reliant. As borders become more secure, terrorist groups must increasingly inspire lone wolf terrorists if groups are to project their power abroad. Fifth, the death tolls of well-executed low-tech terrorist attacks are sufficiently large to attract the world-wide attention that religious fundamentalist terrorists seek.

What Is Weapons of Mass Destruction (WMDs) Terrorism?

Technically, WMDs consist of any mine, bomb, or device that can disperse chemicals, biological organisms, or radiation in large enough quantities to kill. There is, surprisingly, no requirement that the loss of life be extensive—the mere application of chemical, biological, radiological, or nuclear (CBRN) substances is enough to qualify a device as a WMD.[14] For example, a terrorist group's attempt to release anthrax, a bacteria, for political purposes is classified as CBRN or WMD terrorism even if no one dies. CBRN terrorist attacks can be small scale, intended for discriminate targeting, or large scale, intended for mass casualties. The use of ricin, a deadly poison made from castor beans, to assassinate a targeted individual for political reasons qualifies as biological terrorism. On March 20, 1995, Aum Shinrikyo's release of sarin gas, a deadly nerve agent, in the Tokyo subway during morning rush hour was intended to murder thousands of people. This subway attack consisted of eleven dispersal devices on five subway trains. Fortunately, only twelve people perished but well over one thousand people were sickened, around seventy seriously.[15]

Nuclear terrorist attacks can involve exploding a nuclear bomb or attacking a nuclear facility. The bomb scenario requires that terrorists either steal or make a bomb. Neither is likely. An attack on a nuclear facility is more feasible and could lead to the release of radiological material. Even more likely is the bombing or hijacking of a truck carrying nuclear waste to a disposal site. Any deployed bomb would have to be sufficiently powerful to pierce reinforced containers surrounding the transported radiological material.

A radiological weapon is a dirty bomb in which an explosive device is used to disperse radiological material. The intent of a dirty bomb is to create long-term adverse economic consequences as the emitted material closes down a portion of a city during the cleanup. The necessary material could be stolen from a university laboratory, a hospital, or a nuclear power plant. The first two venues are softer targets but possess less hazardous material that remains radioactive for a shorter time frame than highly radioactive and deadly plutonium, found at fast-breeder reactors or nuclear weapons plants. A small dirty bomb in the twin ports of Los Angeles and Long Beach, California, could result in $34 billion in damages and the loss of over two hundred thousand jobs for a period of four months.[16]

Chemical attacks may involve nerve agents (sarin and VX), blood agents (hydrogen cyanide), choking agents (chlorine), and blistering agents (mustard gas). Such chemical attacks are most deadly when victims are exposed to high concentrations of these agents in confined areas. Chemical agents kill in various ways, all of which are agonizing. Chemical weapons are the easiest of the CBRN weapons for terrorists to acquire and deploy.[17]

Biological agents also fall into four categories: highly toxic poisons (ricin), viruses (smallpox, viral hemorrhagic fever, and virulent influenzas), bacteria (anthrax), and plagues (black plague and tularemia).[18] The poisons lend themselves to political assassinations, while viruses, bacteria, and plagues can kill thousands or more if a population is exposed and immediate countermeasures are not taken. Vaccines can be used against some viruses, while antibiotics can be used against some plagues and bacteria. The key to limiting deaths from a terrorist biological attack is to stockpile vaccines and antibiotics, and to have a battle plan in place. The Department of Homeland Security (DHS) is stockpiling smallpox vaccine and antibiotics under its biodefense program. Another key to countering such biological attacks is to have air monitors in cities to know of exposures so that vaccines and antibiotics can be administered immediately to the greatest number of at-risk people.

To accomplish mass casualties, biological terrorist attacks require a tremendous degree of sophistication in terms of weaponization so that the bacteria—say, anthrax—can be inhaled in sufficient quantities by the intended victims. The optimum aerosol particle size is one to five microns, which is sufficiently fine to stay airborne for hours and sufficiently light to be dispersed through air-exchange systems in buildings. Apparently, the anthrax letters sent to the media and two US senators in September and October 2001 contained particles in this size range and were highly concentrated (10^{12} spores per gram), leading the authorities to believe that the anthrax had been stolen from a US research laboratory.[19] To this day, the perpetrator has not been caught.

Are Mass-Casualty Attacks Involving WMD Terrorism Likely?

There is no doubt that some CBRN terrorist attacks can be horrific, but many factors work against such attacks becoming common or even episodic. The terrorist group that came the closest to pulling of a mass-casualty chemical attack was Aum Shinrikyo. In June 1994, Aum Shinrikyo released concentrated sarin gas into a block of apartments in Matsumoto, Japan, where three judges slept who were presiding over a civil suit brought against Aum Shinrikyo. At the time of the sarin release, the wind blew the gas back on the seven perpetrators, thus killing them.[20] The intended victims—the judges—were only slightly sickened. After this failed attack, the group was scared of sarin and diluted it greatly in the March 1995 Tokyo subway attack. These actions are why so few people died in the subway attack. Most of the diluted and liquefied sarin soaked into the subway cars' floors and did not get airborne, thus avoiding the planned massive death toll.

One must remember that Aum Shinrikyo was a rather unique terrorist organization. It consisted of ten thousand members, spread throughout Japan.[21] The group had legions of followers in Russia, Germany, the United States, Australia, and elsewhere. Within Aum Shinrikyo, there were physicists, chemists, and engineers, who provided scientific expertise that enabled the group to pursue CBRN terrorism. Aum Shinrikyo was well funded through donations, software sales, and other commercial endeavors. Police raids after the Tokyo subway attack uncovered over a billion dollars of assets. The group was hierarchically organized, which allowed for specialization of labor and communication throughout the organization, necessary for large-scale and complex terrorist attacks. Aum Shinrikyo planned to become self-reliant in the manufacture of assault weapons, ammunitions, and explosives. Allegedly, the group had amassed sufficient sarin to kill over four million people and had acquired an Mi-17 helicopter to spray sarin over Tokyo.[22] Although the group's actions before the 1995 Tokyo subway attack had raised suspicions, Japanese authorities did not have the indisputable evidence required to raid the group's compounds until after the 1995 subway attack.

There are numerous factors that inhibit terrorist groups from engaging in mass-casualty CBRN terrorism. First, the group must confront a serious handling risk, which is well illustrated by the Matsumoto fiasco, where the perpetrators and not the judges died. Second, the required scientific expertise for CBRN attacks is rarely possessed by terrorist groups. Third, the trend to loosely knit groups limits their ability to engage in complex CBRN terrorist attacks. Fourth, since conventional terrorist attacks can, on occasion, result in great carnage, there is no need to incur the cost and risk of CBRN terrorism. Conventional terrorist attacks, intended to kill many people, are often more cost-effective than a CBRN attack. Fifth, a large-scale CBRN incident will result in major retribution by the authorities from the countries of the victims. Just consider the retribution stemming from 9/11 on al-Qaeda and the Taliban, and 9/11 was a conventional terrorist attack! Countries that might sponsor such a CBRN terrorist attack are aware of the retaliatory response that would follow once their role became known. Sixth, the material for some CBRN attacks are difficult to acquire—for example, weaponized anthrax, plutonium, or a nuclear bomb. Seventh, a CBRN terrorist incident may lose constituency support and financing for a terrorist group, especially if the attack indiscriminately kills many, including supporters.

Because of these inhibitors, I do not see large-scale CBRN attacks as likely in the foreseeable future. Many large terrorist groups today, like ISIS, are engaged in a civil war and have difficulty in projecting power abroad, except in terms of small terrorist cells (for example, cells involved in the November 13, 2015, Paris attacks) or lone wolf terrorists. Neither poses a CBRN threat.

Small-scale CBRN attacks are a different matter. During 1988–2004, two studies examine 316 CBRN terrorist attacks worldwide and find the following breakdown: 65.5 percent, chemical; 13.3 percent, biological; 8.2 percent, radiological, 2.5 percent, nuclear, 2.2 percent, combination, and 8.2 percent, unknown.[23] Generally, the nuclear "attacks" or incidents involved attempts to acquire nuclear or fissile material. For the radiological incidents, there were two instances of small dirty bombs, planted by Chechen rebels, that did not explode. During the time period of the data, the average number of deaths per CBRN terrorist incident was half of that associated with conventional terrorist incidents. Deaths per CBRN attack were, thankfully, just 0.5 persons. Religious fundamentalist and nationalist/separatist terrorist groups were not more likely than others to engage in CBRN incidents. In fact, religious cults and groups with a transnational orientation posed the largest threat of small-scale CBRN terrorist incidents.

In particular, any concern should be with respect to small-scale chemical terrorist attacks since they have been more prevalent in the past than other kinds of CBRN attacks. Moreover, a determined terrorist group can acquire the required chemical substance fairly easily. Venues for past chemical and biological terrorist incidents have been rich democratic countries, so that actions by the DHS and local authorities to be prepared for small-scale chemical and biological attacks are prudent. Nevertheless, I do not view such attacks as posing a large worry for the foreseeable future.

What Are the Hot Spots for Future Terrorist Attacks?

In terms of regions, most terrorist attacks over the coming decades will be in the Middle East and North Africa, followed by sub-Saharan Africa and South Asia. The bulk of terrorist attacks will be domestic, such as those against schools by Boko Haram in Nigeria. Transnational terrorist attacks will constitute about 10 to 15 percent of future terrorist attacks. The latter will continue on occasion to be staged in large Western cities, especially capital cities. Westerners will be most at risk when abroad, particularly in the Middle East and North Africa.

The primary perpetrators will continue to be religious fundamentalist terrorists. With a growing US presence in hot spots in the Middle East and Afghanistan, Americans will continue to be a preferred target of transnational terrorist attacks abroad, except on the occasion when a Canadian is mistaken as an American. US drone attacks in the Middle East and South Asia will also encourage terrorists to strike American interests.

What Is the Shape of Terrorism to Come?

In Western industrial countries, borders will be made ever more secure and, as they are, terrorist groups such as ISIS and AQAP will appeal to new followers to commit terrorist acts using everyday objects such as knives, cars, trucks, and guns. This was the case of Faisal Mohammad, an eighteen-year-old student at the University of California, Merced, who stabbed four fellow students on November 4, 2015. Apparently, Mohammad had been inspired by ISIS-posted terrorist propaganda on the Internet.[24] There are many other instances worldwide of such lone wolf terrorists. As terrorist groups experience greater difficulty in dispatching their trained operatives abroad, these groups will resort to more such web-inspired converts. This will also be true as groups lose territory in their home base.

Terrorists will change their tactics as technology advances. The next big tactical innovation will involve drone attacks, where one or more drones are fitted with compact, but powerful, bombs that can be used to disperse shrapnel on a crowd at stadiums, public parks, or other outdoor public gatherings. ISIS has already deployed drones on the battlefield in Syria and Iraq against opposition forces. It is only a matter of time before drones are engineered for terrorist attacks. Such an attack would likely involve multiple drones, so that the first explosion would divert the attention of the authorities before second and possibly third waves of drones target exits where the largest crowds would be funneled by the initial blast.

I anticipate that the United States will experience suicide bombings in shopping malls, on subways, and other public places. Europe has already experienced such attacks in Brussels, London, Paris, Moscow, and Istanbul. Because such suicide bombings are cheap, grab attention, and generate widespread anxiety, they will surely spread to the United States given its increasing presence in the Middle East and Afghanistan. These suicide attacks can breach first and second layers of security so that armed assailants can then kill scores of people. This means that multiple layers of security must be instituted at airports and other likely targets. For example, the first layer of screening will be at the entrance to the terminal, as is true in some countries.

On June 28, 2016, one armed assailant got through the security checkpoint at Istanbul Atatürk International Airport after a fellow terrorist detonated his suicide vest at the checkpoint. This method is sure to be copied in future airport attacks. In the Atatürk Airport attack 45 people died and 239 were injured.[25] Other terrorist attacks in Europe in recent years (for example, the November 13, 2015, Paris attacks) combined suicide bombings and armed attacks at multiple locations as a way of increasing the body counts and anxiety. Such simultaneous attacks hark back to the Abu Nidal Organization's attacks on the Rome and Vienna airports on December 27, 1985, with the suicide bombing component now thrown in to allow assailants to pass fortified entry points. To know what innovations are to come, the authorities only need to read major terrorist groups' online magazines and manuals and see what tactics are employed in current civil wars.

Terrorists will continue to favor transportation as their preferred mass-casualty venue. Given the ever-tightening security at airports, terrorists will increasingly target boats, trains, and subways. Past suicide bombings on subways include London on July 7, 2005 (three bombings), Moscow on March 29, 2010 (two bombings), and Brussels on March 22, 2016 (one bombing on the day of the Brussels airport attack). In the United States, there is surprisingly little security at most major train stations. It is only a matter of time before terrorist attacks shift to this soft target.

To understand terrorists' fixation on targeting transportation, one only needs to imagine the unbelievable horrors on Pan Am Flight 103 and later on the ground in Lockerbie, Scotland, on December 21, 1988. Within seconds, 259 bodies, some recognizable and some not, rained on the small town of Lockerbie at 7:03 p.m., a little over half a minute after the plane blew apart at 7:02 p.m. at an altitude of thirty-one thousand feet. According to an account reconstructed in *The Guardian*: "Before anyone (on board) realized what was happening, the electricity went out and it became completely dark. Several fractions of a second later, large sections of the forward fuselage were ripped away. The nose of the plane then broke off and fell towards the right into the depths. The people on board . . . were hit with a shock wave of cold, noise and dark. . . . From one second to the next, conditions had suddenly become similar to those on the peak of Mount Everest. . . . The passengers lost consciousness while the main body of the

Maid of the Seas tipped forward."[26] I have tried to imagine my thoughts just prior to losing consciousness had I been aboard the doomed airliner. Conceivably, I would have first thought that this is it, and that I would not be seeing my loved ones at Christmas. In a state of shock, I would have instinctively fought for consciousness and my last living breath, oblivious to the elements. Terrorism would never have entered my mind before the complete silence and then blackness.

The terror in Lockerbie was equally horrific, as 290 tons of wreckage, debris, and fuel fell at half the speed of sound with a deafening roar on the center of the town. A large portion of the plane instantly obliterated four houses on Sherwood Crescent. Again, according to *The Guardian*: "The earthquake monitoring centre in Eskdalemuir, 14 km away, registered a tremor of 1.6 on the Richter scale. The middle part of the plane, complete with the wings, tore a gash into the earth that was 47 metres long and a metre deep; 1,500 tons of earth was lifted into the air and eventually blocked traffic on the A74."[27] In Lockerbie, there were explosions and walls of fire. In total, eleven people died on the ground. The people of Lockerbie that night witnessed hell on earth with no immediate inkling that this was terrorism. Their quiet way of life had been shattered.

Pan Am 103 was one past face of terrorism in its ugliest possible form. Other forms of terrorism have played out since Pan Am 103 in armed attacks, suicide attacks, and bombings perpetrated on unsuspecting victims.

NOTES

Chapter 1

1. Walter Enders and Todd Sandler (2012), *The Political Economy of Terrorism*, 2nd ed. (New York: Cambridge University Press).
2. Edward F. Mickolus (1989), "What Constitutes State Support to Terrorists?" *Terrorism and Political Violence* 1 (3), 287–293.
3. Bruce Hoffman (2006), *Inside Terrorism*, revised ed. (New York: Columbia University Press).
4. On the average carnage of suicide bombings, see Robert A. Pape (2005), *Dying to Win: The Strategic Logic of Suicide Terrorism* (New York: Random House), and Ami Pedahzur (2005), *Suicide Terrorism* (Malden, MA: Polity Press). On the carnage of a conventional attack, see Enders and Sandler, *The Political Economy of Terrorism*.
5. Patrick T. Brandt, Justin George, and Todd Sandler (2016), "Why Concessions Should Not Be Made to Terrorist Kidnappers," *European Journal of Political Economy* 44, 41–52.
6. A threat is a promise of a future attack, while a hoax is a false claim of a past attack. The latter includes phoning the authorities that a bomb is on a plane that just took off when no bomb is aboard.
7. The data for Figure 1.1 comes from Edward F. Mickolus, Todd Sandler, Jean M. Murdock, and Peter Flemming (2016), *International Terrorism: Attributes of Terrorist Events, 1968–2015* (ITERATE) (Pointe Vedra, FL: Vinyard Software). Transnational hostage incidents involve two or more countries owing to the nationalities of the victims or perpetrators.

8. On the distinction between domestic and transnational terrorism
   see Walter Enders, Todd Sandler, and Khusrav Gaibulloev (2011),
   "Domestic versus Transnational Terrorism: Data, Decomposition,
   and Dynamics," *Journal of Peace Research* 48 (3), 355–371, and
   Todd Sandler (2010), "Terrorism Shocks: Domestic versus
   Transnational Responses," *Studies in Conflict & Terrorism* 33 (10),
   893–910.

9. On the relative economic influences of domestic and
   transnational terrorism, see Subhayu Bandyopadhyay, Todd
   Sandler, and Javed Younas (2014), "Foreign Direct Investment,
   Aid, and Terrorism," *Oxford Economic Papers* 66 (1), 25–50,
   and Khusrav Gaibulloev and Todd Sandler (2008), "Growth
   Consequences of Terrorism in Western Europe," *Kyklos* 61 (3),
   411–424.

10. On the DHS budget see Enders and Sandler, *The Political Economy
    of Terrorism*, chapter 11, and US DHS (2016), Budget-in-Brief
    Fiscal Year 2017, https://www.dhs.gov/sites/default/files/
    publications/FY2017_BIB.pdf.

11. Axel Dreher and Andreas Fuchs (2011), "Does Terror Increase
    Aid?" *Public Choice* 149 (3–4), 337–363, and Robert K. Fleck and
    Christopher Kilby (2010), "Changing Aid Regimes? US Foreign
    Aid from the Cold War to War on Terror," *Journal of Development
    Economics* 91 (1), 185–197.

12. Hoffman, *Inside Terrorism* discusses the differences between these
    terrorist groups. Also see Seth G. Jones and Martin C. Libicki
    (2008), *How Terrorist Groups End: Lessons for Countering al Qa'ida*
    (Santa Monica, CA: Rand). These percentages are pulled from
    ITERATE.

13. John Mueller (2004), "A False Sense of Insecurity," *Regulation* 27
    (3), 42–46.

14. Mueller, "A False Sense of Insecurity," and Todd Sandler, Daniel
    G. Arce, and Walter Enders (2009), "Transnational Terrorism," in
    Global Crises, Global Solutions, 2nd ed., edited by Bjørn Lomborg,
    pp. 516–562 (Cambridge: Cambridge University Press).

15. On these distinctions, see Todd Sandler and Keith Hartley (1995),
    The Economics of Defense (Cambridge: Cambridge University
    Press), and Nicholas Sambanis (2008), "Terrorism and Civil
    War," in *Terrorism, Economic Development and Political Openness*,
    edited by Philip Keefer and Norma Loayza, pp. 174–206
    (New York: Cambridge University Press). On the use of terrorism

in civil wars, see Michael E. Findley and Joseph K. Young (2012), "Terrorism and Civil War: A Spatial and Temporal Approach to a Conceptual Problem," *Perspectives on Politics* 10 (2), 285–305, and Khusrav Gaibulloev, James A. Piazza, and Todd Sandler (2017), "Regime Types and Terrorism," *International Organization* 71 (3), 491–522.

16. David C. Rapoport (1984), "Fear and Trembling: Terrorism in Three Religious Traditions," *American Political Science Review* 78 (3), 658–677.

17. https://en.wikipedia.org/wiki/Assassination_of_William_McKinley.

18. https://en.wikipedia.org/wiki/Wall_Street_bombing.

19. David C. Rapoport (2004), "Modern Terror: The Four Waves," in *Attacking Terrorism: Elements of a Grand Strategy*, edited by Audrey Kurth Cronin and James M. Ludes, pp. 46–73 (Washington, DC: Georgetown University Press).

20. Jones and Libicki, *How Terrorist Groups End.*

21. Edward F. Mickolus (1980), *Transnational Terrorism: A Chronology of Events, 1968–1979* (Westport, CT: Greenwood Press).

22. The data for Figure 1.2 come from Mickolus et al., *ITERATE.*

23. GTD data come from the National Consortium for the Study of Terrorism and Responses to Terrorism (START) (2016), *Global Terrorism Database* (College Park, MD: University of Maryland) at www.start.umd.edu/gtd/. The division of GTD data into domestic and transnational terrorism incidents is engineered by Enders, Sandler, and Gaibulloev, "Domestic versus Transnational Terrorism." Also see Bandyopadhyay, Sandler, and Younas, "Foreign Direct Investment, Aid and Terrorism," and Khusrav Gaibulloev, Todd Sandler, and Charlinda Santifort (2012), "Assessing the Evolving Threat of Terrorism," *Global Policy* 3 (2), 135–144.

24. Todd Sandler and Harvey E. Lapan (1988), "The Calculus of Dissent: An Analysis of Terrorists' Choice of Targets," *Syntheses* 76 (2), 245–261, and Todd Sandler and Kevin Siqueira (2006), "Global Terrorism: Deterrence versus Preemption," *Canadian Journal of Economics* 50 (4), 1370–1387.

25. Harvey E. Lapan and Todd Sandler (1993), "Terrorism and Signalling," *European Journal of Political Economy* 9 (3), 383–397.

26. On the success of suicide campaigns, see Robert A. Pape (2003), "The Strategic Logic of Suicide Terrorism," *American Political*

Science Review 97 (3), 343–361. On these twenty-eight campaigns, see Max Abrahms (2006), "Why Terrorism Does Not Work," *International Security* 31 (2), 42–78. The study with over five hundred terrorist groups is Khusrav Gaibulloev and Todd Sandler (2014), "An Empirical Analysis of Alternative Ways That Terrorist Groups End," *Public Choice* 160 (1–2), 25–44.

Chapter 2

1. See the following sources on causes of terrorism: Walter Enders and Todd Sandler (2012), *The Political Economy of Terrorism*, 2nd ed. (New York: Cambridge University Press), Bruce Hoffman (2006), *Inside Terrorism*, revised ed. (New York: Columbia University Press), James A. Piazza (2011), "Poverty, Minority Economic Discrimination and Domestic Terrorism," *Journal of Peace Research* 48 (3), 339–353, Jessica Stern (2003), *Terror in the Name of God: Why Religious Militants Kill* (New York: HarperCollins), and Paul Wilkinson (2001), *Terrorism versus Democracy: The Liberal State Response* (London: Frank Cass).

2. Quoted in Alan B. Krueger and Jitka Malečková (2003), "Education, Poverty, and Terrorism: Is There a Causal Connection?," *Journal of Economic Perspectives* 17 (4), 119–144.

3. Jean-Paul Azam and Alexandra Delacroix (2006), "Aid and the Delegated Fight against Terrorism," *Review of Development Economics* 10 (2), 330–344, Jean-Paul Azam and Véronique Thelen (2010), "Foreign Aid versus Military Intervention in the War on Terror," *Journal of Conflict Resolution* 54 (2), 237–261, Axel Dreher and Andreas Fuchs (2011), "Does Terror Increase Aid?," *Public Choice* 149 (3–4), 337–363, and Robert K. Fleck and Christopher Kilby (2010), "Changing Aid Regimes? US Foreign Aid from the Cold War to War on Terror," *Journal of Development Economics* 91 (1), 185–197.

4. Burcu Savun and Brian J. Phillips (2009), "Democracy, Foreign Policy, and Terrorism," *Journal of Conflict Resolution* 53 (6), 878–904.

5. On globalization and terrorism, see Quan Li and Drew Schaub (2004), "Economic Globalization and Transnational Terrorism," *Journal of Conflict Resolution* 48 (2), 230–258, and Marc Sageman (2008), *Leaderless Jihad: Terror Networks in the Twenty-First Century* (Philadelphia, PA: University of Pennsylvania Press).

6. The text's account of the Munich Olympics hostage incident is derived from Hoffman, *Inside Terrorism*, pp. 66–71, and Edward F. Mickolus (1980), *Transnational Terrorism: A Chronology of Events, 1968–1979* (Westport, CT: Greenwood Press).

7. Hoffman, *Inside Terrorism*, pp. 68–69.

8. See Martin Gassebner and Simon Luechinger (2011), "Lock, Stock and Barrel: A Comprehensive Assessment of Determinants of Terror," *Public Choice* 149 (3–4), 235–261, and Li and Schaub, "Economic Globalization and Transnational Terrorism." Other relevant articles include Konstantinos Drakos and Andreas Gofas (2006), "In Search of the Average Transnational Terrorist Attack Venue," *Defence and Peace Economics* 17 (2), 73–93, and Khusrav Gaibulloev, James A. Piazza, and Todd Sandler (2017), "Regime Types and Terrorism," *International Organization* 71 (3), 491–522.

9. President Bush's view was echoed by the former US secretary of state Colin Powell in a 2002 State Department memorandum and, years later, by former US secretary of state John Kerry at a Vatican meeting in 2014. See Maayan Jaffe-Hoffman (2016), "Does Poverty Motivate Palestinian Terror?" http:// www.charismanews.com/opinion/standing-with-Israel/ 57290-does-poverty-motivate-palestinian-terror.

10. Claude Berrebi (2007), "Evidence about the Link between Education, Poverty and Terrorism among Palestinians," *Peace Economics, Peace Science, and Public Policy* 13 (1), 1–36, and Krueger and Malečková, "Education, Poverty, and Terrorism." The latter is the prominent study referred to in the text. Also see Alberto Abadie (2006), "Poverty, Political Freedom and the Roots of Terrorism," *American Economic Review* 96 (2), 50–56.

11. Representative articles that display a positive relationship between income per capita and poverty include Subhayu Bandyopadhyay and Javed Younas (2011), "Poverty, Political Freedom, and the Roots of Terrorism in Developing Countries: An Empirical Assessment," *Economics Letters* 112 (2), 171–176, S. Brock Blomberg, Gregory D. Hess, and Akila Weerapana (2004), "Economic Conditions and Terrorism," *European Journal of Political Economy* 20 (2), 463–478, and Gassebner and Luechinger, "Lock, Stock, and Barrel." A representative article that finds a negative relationship between income per capita and terrorism is Li and Schaub, "Economic Globalization and Transnational Terrorism." Finally,

representative articles that indicate no relationship between income per capita and poverty include Abadie, "Poverty, Political Freedom and the Roots of Terrorism" and Krueger and Malečková, "Education, Poverty, and Terrorism."

12. This paragraph is referring to the study by Walter Enders, Gary A. Hoover, and Todd Sandler (2016), "The Changing Nonlinear Relationship between Income and Terrorism," *Journal of Conflict Resolution* 60 (2), 195–225.

13. Efraim Benmelech and Claude Berrebi (2007), "Human Capital and the Productivity of Suicide Bombers," *Journal of Economic Perspectives* 21 (2), 223–238.

14. See, for example, Gassebner and Luechinger, "Lock, Stock, and Barrel."

15. Piazza, "Poverty, Minority Economic Discrimination and Domestic Terrorism."

16. Matthias Basedau, Jonathan Fox, Jan H. Pierskalla, Georg Strüver, and Johannes Vüllers (2017), "Does Discrimination Breed Grievances—and Do Grievances Breed Violence? New Evidence from an Analysis of Religious Minorities in Developing Countries," *Conflict Management and Peace Science* 34 (3), 217–239.

17. Mujib Mashal, Fahim Abed, and Jawad Sukhanyar (2017), "Deadly Bombing in Kabul Is One of the Afghan War's Worst Strikes," http://www.nytimes.com/2017/05/31/world/asia/kabul-explosion-afghanistan.html?_r=1, Ehsan Popalzai, Laura Smith-Spark, and Faith Karimi (2017), "Kabul Blast: Attack Kills 90 Near Diplomatic Area in Afghanistan," www.cnn.com/2017/05/31/asia/kabul-explosion-hits-diplomatic-area/, and Rod Nordland (2017), "Death Toll in Kabul Bombing Has Hit 150, Afghan President Says," https://www.nytimes.com/2017/06/06/world/asia/kabul-bombing-death-toll-increases.html?-r=0.

18. Russell Goldman (2017), "ISIS Blasts Kill Dozens at Family Gatherings, This Time in Iraq," *New York Times*, May 30, https://nytimes.com/2017/05/30/world/middleeast/isis-attacks-baghdad-iraq.html?_r=0.

19. Enders and Sandler, *The Political Economy of Terrorism*, pp. 55–59.

20. Mickolus, *Transnational Terrorism*, p. 574, and Edward F. Mickolus and Susan L. Simmons (2005), *Terrorism, 2002–2004: A Chronology* (Westport, CT: Praeger Security International).

21. Savun and Phillips, "Democracy, Foreign Policy, and Terrorism," find a linkage between foreign policy and transnational terrorism for a limited number of years; however, Gaibulloev, Piazza, and Sandler, "Regime Types and Terrorism," do not uncover a linkage between foreign policy and transnational terrorism for a larger sample period and using more sophisticated empirical methods.

22. Edward Mickolus (2016), *Terrorism 2013–2015: A Worldwide Chronology* (Jefferson, NC: McFarland), and Edward Mickolus (2017), *Terrorism Worldwide, 2016* (Jefferson, NC: McFarland).

23. Axel Dreher, Martin Gassebner, and Paul Schaudt (2017), "The Effect of Migration on Terror—Made at Home or Imported from Abroad?," unpublished manuscript.

24. On strategic factors, see William L. Eubank and Leonard B. Weinberg (1994), "Does Democracy Encourage Terrorism?," *Terrorism and Political Violence* 13 (1), 155–164, Joe Eyerman (1998), "Terrorism and Democratic States: Soft Targets or Accessible Systems?," *International Interactions* 24 (2), 151–170, Gaibulloev, Piazza, and Sandler, "Regime Types and Terrorism," and Quan Li (2005), "Does Democracy Promote Transnational Terrorist Incidents?," *Journal of Conflict Resolution* 49 (2), 278–297.

25. On Northwest Airlines Flight 305, see Mickolus, *Transnational Terrorism*, pp. 287–288, and William M. Landes (1978), "An Economic Study of US Aircraft Hijackings, 1961–1976," *Journal of Law and Economics* 21 (1), 1–31.

26. On political access and its negative influence on terrorism, see Eyerman, "Terrorism and Democratic States," Lawrence C. Hamilton and James D. Hamilton (1983), "Dynamics of Terrorism," *International Studies Quarterly* 27 (1), 39–54, Gaibulloev, Piazza, and Sandler "Regime Types and Terrorism," and Li, "Does Democracy Promote Transnational Terrorist Incidents?."

27. Enders and Sandler, *The Political Economy of Terrorism*, chapter 11.

28. Mickolus and Simmons, *Terrorism, 2002–2004*.

29. Gaibulloev, Piazza, and Sandler, "Regime Types and Terrorism."

30. The account of this incident is taken from Edward F. Mickolus, Todd Sandler, and Jean M. Murdock (1989), *International Terrorism in the 1980s: A Chronology of Events*, vol. 2, *1984–1987* (Ames, IA: Iowa State University Press).

31. Enders and Sandler, *The Political Economy of Terrorism*.

Chapter 3

1. On definitions of terrorist groups, see Brian J. Phillips (2015), "What Is a Terrorist Group? Conceptual Issues and Empirical Implications," *Terrorism and Political Violence* 27 (2), 225–242.
2. Edward F. Mickolus, Todd Sandler, and Jean M. Murdock (1989), *International Terrorism in the 1980s: A Chronology of Events*, vol. 2, *1984–1987* (Ames, IA: Iowa State University Press), pp. 325–328. Details of these two airport attacks are taken from this source.
3. On such group distinctions, see Eli Berman (2009), *Radical, Religious, and Violent: The New Economics of Terrorism* (Cambridge, MA: MIT Press), Audrey K. Cronin (2006), "How al-Qaida Ends: The Decline and Demise of Terrorist Groups," *International Security* 31 (1), 7–48, Audrey K. Cronin (2009), *How Terrorism Ends: Understanding the Decline and Demise of Terrorist Campaigns* (Princeton, NJ: Princeton University Press), Luis de la Calle and Ignacio Sánchez-Cuenca (2012), "Rebels without a Territory: An Analysis of Nonterritorial Conflicts in the World, 1970–1997," *Journal of Conflict Resolution* 56 (4), 580–603, Walter Enders and Todd Sandler (2012), *The Political Economy of Terrorism*, 2nd ed. (New York: Cambridge University Press), William L. Eubank and Leonard B. Weinberg (1994), "Does Democracy Encourage Terrorism?," *Terrorism and Political Violence* 6 (4), 155–164, and Phillips, "What Is a Terrorist Group?"
4. Cronin, "How al-Qaida Ends," and Seth G. Jones and Martin C. Libicki (2008), *How Terrorist Groups End: Lessons for Countering al Qa'ida* (Santa Monica, CA: Rand).
5. Edward Mickolus (2017), *Terrorism Worldwide, 2016* (Jefferson, NC: McFarland).
6. Khusrav Gaibulloev and Todd Sandler (2013), "Determinants of the Demise of Terrorist Organizations," *Southern Economic Journal* 79 (4), 774–792.
7. Bruce Hoffman (2006), *Inside Terrorism*, revised ed. (New York: Columbia University Press), and David C. Rapoport (2004), "Modern Terror: The Four Waves," in *Attacking Terrorism: Elements of a Grand Strategy*, edited by Audrey K. Cronin and James M. Ludes, pp. 46–73 (Washington, DC: Georgetown University Press).
8. Enders and Sandler, *The Political Economy of Terrorism*, pp. 56–58, and Hoffman, *Inside Terrorism*.

9. S. Brock Blomberg, Khusrav Gaibulloev, and Todd Sandler (2011), "Terrorist Group Survival: Ideology, Tactics, and Base of Operations," *Public Choice* 149 (3–4), 441–463, Gaibulloev and Sandler, "Determinants of the Demise of Terrorist Organizations," Khusrav Gaibulloev and Todd Sandler (2014), "An Empirical Analysis of Alternative Ways That Terrorist Groups End," *Public Choice* 160 (1–2), 25–44, and Jones and Libicki, *How Terrorist Groups End.*

10. Khusrav Gaibulloev and Todd Sandler (2017), "What We Have Learned about Terrorism since 9/11," unpublished manuscript, Center for Global Collective Action, University of Texas at Dallas, Richardson, TX.

11. Martha Crenshaw (1981), "The Causes of Terrorism," *Comparative Politics* 13 (4), 379–399, and Hoffman, *Inside Terrorism.*

12. This statement is based on terrorists' interviews and profiles published in Marc Sageman (2004), *Understanding Terror Networks* (Philadelphia, PA: University of Pennsylvania Press), and Marc Sageman (2008), *Leaderless Jihad: Terror Networks in the Twenty-First Century* (Philadelphia, PA: University of Pennsylvania Press).

13. Ronald Wintrobe (2006), "Extremism, Suicide Terror, and Authoritarianism," *Public Choice* 128 (1), 169–195.

14. Eli Berman (2000), "Sect, Subsidy and Sacrifice: An Economist's View of Ultra-Orthodox Jews," *Quarterly Journal of Economics* 115 (3), 905–953, Eli Berman (2009), *Radical, Religious, and Violent: The New Economics of Terrorism* (Cambridge, MA: MIT Press), R. Laurence Iannaccone (1992), "Sacrifice and Stigma: Reducing Free-Riding in Cults, Communes, and Other Collectives," *Journal of Political Economy* 100 (2), 271–291, and R. Laurence Iannaccone and Eli Berman (2006), "Religious Extremism: The Good, the Bad, and the Deadly," *Public Choice* 128 (1–2), 109–129.

15. Daniel G. Arce and Todd Sandler (2010), "Terrorist Spectaculars: Backlash Attacks and the Focus of Intelligence," *Journal of Conflict Resolution* 54 (2), 354–373, B. Peter Rosendorff and Todd Sandler (2004), "Too Much of a Good Thing? The Proactive Response Dilemma," *Journal of Conflict Resolution* 48 (5), 657–671, B. Peter Rosendorff and Todd Sandler (2010), "Suicide Terrorism and the Backlash Effect," *Defence and Peace Economics* 21 (5–6), 443–457, and Kevin Siqueira and Todd Sandler

(2007), "Terrorist Backlash, Terrorism Mitigation, and Policy Delegation," *Journal of Public Economics* 91 (9), 1800–1815.

16. Eli Berman and David D. Laitin (2008), "Religion, Terrorism, and Public Clubs: Testing the Club Model," *Journal of Public Economics* 92 (9–10), 1942–1967.

17. Enders and Sandler, *The Political Economy of Terrorism*, pp. 57–59, Robert A. Pape (2003), "The Strategic Logic of Suicide Terrorism," *American Political Science Review* 97 (3), 343–361, and Robert A. Pape (2005), *Dying to Win: The Strategic Logic of Suicide Terrorism* (New York: Random House).

18. Edward Mickolus and Susan L. Simmons (2002), *Terrorism 1996–2001: A Chronology* (Westport, CT: Greenwood Press).

19. Pape, "The Strategic Logic of Suicide Terrorism." See Assaf Moghadam (2006), "Suicide Terrorism, Occupation, and the Globalization of Martyrdom: A Critique of *Dying to Win*," *Studies in Conflict & Terrorism* 29 (8), 707–727 for a contrary viewpoint.

20. Berman, *Radical, Religious, and Violent*, and Efraim Benmelech and Claude Berrebi (2007), "Human Capital and the Productivity of Suicide Bombers," *Journal of Economic Perspectives* 21 (2), 223–238.

21. Mark Basile (2004), "Going to the Source: Why Al Qaeda's Financial Network Is Likely to Withstand the Current War on Terrorist Financing," *Studies in Conflict & Terrorism* 27 (3), 169–185, and Matthew Levitt (2003), "Stemming the Flow of Terrorist Financing: Practical and Conceptual Challenges," *Fletcher Forum of World Affairs* 27 (1), 59–70.

22. On state sponsorship, see Edward F. Mickolus (1989), "What Constitutes State Support to Terrorism?," *Terrorism and Political Violence* 1 (3), 287–293. On the era of state sponsorship, see Hoffman, *Inside Terrorism*, pp. 258–263.

23. Hoffman, *Inside Terrorism*, Mickolus, Sandler, and Murdock, *International Terrorism in the 1980s: A Chronology of Events*, vols. 1 and 2, and Edward F. Mickolus (1993), *Terrorism, 1988–1991: A Chronology of Events and a Selectively Annotated Bibliography* (Westport, CT: Greenwood Press).

24. David B. Carter (2012), "A Blessing or a Curse? State Support for Terrorist Groups," *International Organization* 66 (1), 129–151. Also see Navin A. Bapat (2007), "The Internationalization of Terrorist Campaigns," *Conflict Management and Peace Science* 24 (4), 265–280, and Navin A. Bapat (2011), "Transnational Terrorism, US

Military Aid, and the Incentive to Misrepresent," *Journal of Peace Research* 48 (3), 303–318.

25. Cronin, "How al-Qaida Ends," Cronin, *How Terrorism Ends*, and Jones and Libicki, *How Terrorist Groups End*.

26. Enders and Sandler, *The Political Economy of Terrorism*, pp. 20–21.

27. Jones and Libicki, *How Terrorist Groups End*.

28. Brian J. Phillips (forthcoming), "Do 90 Percent of Terrorist Groups Last Less Than a Year? Updating the Conventional Wisdom," *Terrorism and Political Violence*. On one-hit wonders, see S. Brock Blomberg, Rozlyn C. Engel, and Reid Sawyer (2010), "On the Duration and Sustainability of Transnational Terrorist Organizations," *Journal of Conflict Resolution* 54 (2), 303–330.

29. David C. Rapoport (1992), "Terrorism," in *Encyclopedia of Government and Politics*, vol. 2, edited by Mary Hawkesworth and Maurice Kogan (London: Routledge).

30. The reported findings come from the following sources: Blomberg, Gaibulloev, and Sandler, "Terrorist Group Survival," Gaibulloev and Sandler, "Determinants of the Demise of Terrorist Organizations," Jones and Libicki, *How Terrorist Groups End*, Brian J. Phillips (2014), "Terrorist Group Cooperation and Longevity," *International Studies Quarterly* 58 (2), 336–347, and Brian J. Phillips (2015), "Enemies with Benefits: Violent Rivalry and Terrorist Group Longevity," *Journal of Peace Research* 52 (11), 62–75.

31. The findings here draw from Gaibulloev and Sandler, "An Empirical Analysis of Alternative Ways That Terrorist Groups End."

32. Walter Enders and Paan Jindapon (2010), "Network Externalities and the Structure of Terror Networks," *Journal of Conflict Resolution* 54 (2), 262–280, and Walter Enders and Xuejuan Su (2007), "Rational Terrorists and Optimal Network Structure," *Journal of Conflict Resolution* 51 (1), 33–57.

33. Information in this paragraph derives from the fascinating analysis of terrorists' mindset given in Hoffman, *Inside Terrorism*, p. 350.

34. Edward F. Mickolus (1980), *Transnational Terrorism: A Chronology of Events 1968–1979* (Westport, CT: Greenwood Press).

35. Kevin Siqueira (2005), "Political and Militant Wings within Dissident Movements and Organizations," *Journal of Conflict Resolution* 49 (2), 218–236.

36. Jacob N. Shapiro (2007), "Terrorist Organizations' Vulnerabilities and Inefficiencies," in *Terrorism Financing and State Responses: A Comparative Perspective*, edited by Jeanne K. Giraldo and Harold A. Trinkunas, pp. 56–71 (Stanford, CA: Stanford University Press), Jacob N. Shapiro (2013), *The Terrorist's Dilemma: Managing Violent Covert Organizations* (Princeton, NJ: Princeton University Press), and Jacob N. Shapiro and David A. Siegel (2007), "Underfunding in Terrorist Organizations," *International Studies Quarterly* 51 (2), 405–429.

37. See Shapiro, *The Terrorist's Dilemma*.

38. Edward Mickolus and Susan L. Simmons (1997), *Terrorism 1992–1995: A Chronology of Events and a Selectively Annotated Bibliography* (Westport, CT: Greenwood Press).

Chapter 4

1. John Arquilla and David Ronfeldt (eds.) (2001), *Networks and Netwars* (Santa Monica, CA: Rand), Walter Enders and Paan Jindapon (2010), "Network Externalities and the Structure of Terror Networks," *Journal of Conflict Resolution* 54 (2), 262–280, and Marc Sageman (2008), *Leaderless Jihad: Terror Networks in the Twenty-First Century* (Philadelphia, PA: University of Pennsylvania Press).

2. Walter Enders and Todd Sandler (2012), *The Political Economy of Terrorism*, 2nd ed. (New York: Cambridge University Press), and Matthew Levitt (2003), "Stemming the Flow of Terrorist Financing: Practical and Conceptual Challenges," *Fletcher Forum of World Affairs* 27 (1), 59–70.

3. Daniel Jacobson and Edward H. Kaplan (2007), "Suicide Bombings and Targeted Killings in (Counter-) Terror Games," *Journal of Conflict Resolution* 51 (5), 772–792, Edward F. Mickolus and Susan L. Simmons (2005), *Terrorism, 2002–2004: A Chronology* (Westport, CT: Praeger Security International), and Asaf Zussman and Noam Zussman (2006), "Assassinations: Evaluating the Effectiveness of an Israeli Counterterrorism Policy Using Stock Market Data," *Journal of Economic Perspectives* 20 (2), 193–206.

4. Edward F. Mickolus and Susan L. Simmons (1997), *Terrorism, 1992–1995: A Chronology of Events and a Selectively Annotated Bibliography* (Westport, CT: Greenwood Press).

5. Walter Enders and Todd Sandler (1993), "The Effectiveness of Anti-terrorism Policies: A Vector-Autoregression-Intervention

Analysis," *American Political Science Review* 87 (4), 829–844, and William M. Landes (1978), "An Economic Study of US Aircraft Hijackings, 1961–1976," *Journal of Law and Economics* 21 (1), 1–31. Also see Walter Enders, Todd Sandler, and Jon Cauley (1990), "UN Conventions, Technology, and Retaliation in the Fight against Terrorism: An Econometric Evaluation," *Terrorism and Political Violence* 2 (1), 83–105.

6. Robert Powell (2007), "Defending against Terrorist Attacks with Limited Resources," *American Political Science Review* 101 (3), 527–541.

7. Landes, "An Economic Study of US Aircraft Hijackings, 1961–1976."

8. There is a rich literature on the underprovision of proactive counterterrorism measures; see, for example, the following: Daniel G. Arce and Todd Sandler (2005), "Counterterrorism: A Game-Theoretic Analysis," *Journal of Conflict Resolution* 49 (2), 183–200, Ethan Bueno de Mesquita (2007), "Politics and the Suboptimal Provision of Counterterror," *International Organization* 61 (1), 9–36, Andre Rossi de Oliveira, João Ricardo Faria, and Emilson C. D. Silva (2017), "Transnational Terrorism: Externalities and Coalition Formation," *Journal of Conflict Resolution*, DOI: 10.1177/0022002716660586, forthcoming, Todd Sandler and Harvey E. Lapan (1988), "The Calculus of Dissent: An Analysis of Terrorists' Choice of Targets," *Synthese* 76 (2), 245–261, and Todd Sandler and Kevin Siqueira (2006), "Global Terrorism: Deterrence versus Preemption," *Canadian Journal of Economics* 50 (4), 1370–1387.

9. Enders and Sandler, *The Political Economy of Terrorism*.

10. On backlash, see the following: Daniel G. Arce and Todd Sandler (2010), "Terrorist Spectaculars: Backlash Attacks and the Focus of Intelligence," *Journal of Conflict Resolution* 54 (2), 354–373, Mia Bloom (2005), *Dying to Kill: The Allure of Suicide Terror* (New York: Columbia University Press), B. Peter Rosendorff and Todd Sandler (2004), "Too Much of a Good Thing? The Proactive Response Dilemma," *Journal of Conflict Resolution* 48 (5), 657–671, and Kevin Siqueira and Todd Sandler (2007), "Terrorist Backlash, Terrorism Mitigation, and Policy Delegation," *Journal of Public Economics* 91 (9), 1800–1815.

11. Bruce Hoffman (2006), *Inside Terrorism*, revised ed. (New York: Columbia University Press), pp. 53–61.

12. Walter Enders and Todd Sandler (2006), "Distribution of Transnational Terrorism among Countries by Income Classes and Geography after 9/11," *International Studies Quarterly* 50 (2), 367–393, and Enders and Sandler, *The Political Economy of Terrorism*.

13. On this asymmetry, see Arce and Sandler, "Counterterrorism," Enders and Sandler, *The Political Economy of Terrorism*, Todd Sandler (2003), "Collective Action and Transnational Terrorism," *World Economy* 26 (6), 779–802, Todd Sandler (2005), "Collective versus Unilateral Responses to Terrorism," *Public Choice* 124 (1–2), 75–93, Todd Sandler (2010), "Terrorism Shocks: Domestic versus Transnational Responses," *Studies in Conflict & Terrorism* 33 (10), 893–910, and Sandler and Siqueira, "Global Terrorism."

14. S. Brock Blomberg, Khusrav Gaibulloev, and Todd Sandler (2011), "Terrorist Group Survival: Ideology, Tactics, and Base of Operations," *Public Choice* 149 (3–4), 441–463, Khusrav Gaibulloev and Todd Sandler (2013), "Determinants of the Demise of Terrorist Organizations," *Southern Economic Journal* 79 (4), 774–792, and Khusrav Gaibulloev and Todd Sandler (2014), "An Empirical Analysis of Alternative Ways That Terrorist Groups End," *Public Choice* 160 (1–2), 25–44.

15. Subhayu Bandyopadhyay and Todd Sandler (2011), "The Interplay between Preemptive and Defensive Counterterrorism Measures: A Two-Stage Game," *Economica* 78 (3), 546–564, and Eva Cárceles-Poveda and Yair Tauman (2011), "A Strategic Analysis of the War against Transnational Terrorism," *Games and Economic Behavior* 71 (1), 49–65.

16. On target transference, see Patrick T. Brandt and Todd Sandler (2010), "What Do Transnational Terrorists Target? Has It Changed? Are We Safer?" *Journal of Conflict Resolution* 54 (2), 214–236, and Patrick T. Brandt and Todd Sandler (2012), "A Bayesian Poisson Vector Autoregression Model," *Political Analysis* 20 (3), 292–315.

17. Enders and Sandler, "The Effectiveness of Anti-terrorism Policies."

18. Enders and Sandler, *The Political Economy of Terrorism*, p. 91.

19. Eli Berman (2009), *Radical, Religious, and Violent: The New Economics of Terrorism* (Cambridge, MA: MIT Press).

20. Laura Dugan and Erica Chenoweth (2012), "Moving beyond Deterrence: The Effectiveness of Raising the Expected Utility of

Abstaining from Terrorism in Israel," *American Sociological Review* 77 (4), 597–624.

21. Facts about the raid are taken from Edward F. Mickolus, Todd Sandler, and Jean M. Murdock (1989), *International Terrorism in the 1980s: A Chronology of Events*, vol. 2, *1984–1987* (Ames, IA: Iowa State University Press).

22. Enders and Sandler, "The Effectiveness of Anti-terrorism Policies."

23. Bryan Brophy-Baermann and John A. C. Conybeare (1994), "Retaliating against Terrorism: Rational Expectations and the Optimality of Rules versus Discretion," *American Journal of Political Science* 38 (1), 196–210.

24. Marc Sageman (2004), *Understanding Terror Networks* (Philadelphia, PA: University of Pennsylvania Press).

25. See Jean-Paul Azam and Véronique Thelen (2010), "Foreign Aid versus the Military Intervention in the War on Terror," *Journal of Conflict Resolution* 54 (2), 237–261, Subhayu Bandyopadhyay, Todd Sandler, and Javed Younas (2011), "Foreign Aid as Counterterrorism Policy," *Oxford Economic Papers* 63 (3), 423–447, Robert K. Fleck and Christopher Kilby (2010), "Changing Aid Regimes? US Foreign Aid from the Cold War to War of Terror," *Journal of Development Economics* 91 (1), 185–197, and Joseph K. Young and Michael G. Findley (2011), "Can Peace Be Purchased? A Sectoral-Level Analysis of Aid's Influence on Transnational Terrorism," *Public Choice* 149 (3–4), 365–381.

26. Navin A. Bapat (2011), "Transnational Terrorism, US Military Aid, and the Incentive to Misrepresent," *Journal of Peace Research* 48 (3), 303–318.

27. Javier Gardeazabal and Todd Sandler (2015), "INTERPOL's Surveillance Network in Curbing Transnational Terrorism," *Journal of Policy Analysis and Management* 34 (4), 761–780, and Todd Sandler, Daniel G. Arce, and Walter Enders (2011), "An Evaluation of INTERPOL's Cooperative-Based Counterterrorism Linkage," *Journal of Law and Economics* 54 (1), 79–110.

28. See Enders and Sandler, *The Political Economy of Terrorism*. Also see Yonah Alexander, Marjorie Ann Browne, and Allan S. Nanes (1979), *Control of Terrorism: International Documents* (New York: Crane, Russak).

29. See, for example, Paul Wilkinson (1986), *Terrorism and the Liberal State*, revised ed. (London: Macmillan), and Paul Wilkinson

(2001), *Terrorism versus Democracy: The Liberal State Response* (London: Frank Cass).

30. Enders and Sandler, *The Political Economy of Terrorism*, Enders and Sandler, "The Effectiveness of Anti-terrorism Policies," and Enders, Sandler, and Cauley, "UN Conventions, Technology, and Retaliation in the Fight against Terrorism."

31. Enders and Sandler, *The Political Economy of Terrorism*, pp. 194–197, and White House (2003), "Progress Report on the Global War on Terrorism," https://www.state.gov/documents/organization/24268.pdf.

32. Mark Basile (2004), "Going to the Source: Why al Qaida's Financial Network Is Likely to Withstand the Current War on Terrorist Financing," *Studies in Conflict & Terrorism* 27 (3), 169–185.

33. Levitt, "Stemming the Flow of Terrorist Financing."

34. Daniel Byman (2015), *Al Qaeda, the Islamic State, and the Global Jihadist Movement: What Everyone Needs to Know* (New York: Oxford University Press).

35. Enders and Sandler, *The Political Economy of Terrorism*.

36. National Commission on Terrorist Attacks Upon the United States (2004), *The 9/11 Commission Report* (New York: Norton).

37. Enders and Sandler, *The Political Economy of Terrorism*, and Mickolus, Sandler, and Murdock, *International Terrorism in the 1980s*, vol. 2.

38. Patrick T. Brandt and Todd Sandler (2016), "Why Concessions Should Not Be Made to Terrorist Kidnappers," *European Journal of Political Economy* 44, 41–52, and Patrick T. Brandt and Todd Sandler (2009), "Hostage Taking: Understanding Terrorism Event Dynamics," *Journal of Policy Modeling* 31 (5), 758–778.

39. Rukmini Callimachi (2014), "Paying Ransoms, Europe Bankrolls Qaeda Terror," *New York Times*, July 29, http://www.nytimes.com/2014/07/30/world/africa/ransoming-citizens-europe-becomes-al-qaedas-patron.html.

40. Enders and Sandler, *The Political Economy of Terrorism*, chapter 11.

Chapter 5

1. The facts in this paragraph are drawn from Edward F. Mickolus and Susan L. Simmons (2002), *Terrorism 1996–2001: A Chronology* (Westport, CT: Greenwood Press), pp. 262–266, and https://en.wikipedia.org/wiki/USS_Cole_bombing.

2. On asymmetric warfare see David L. Buffaloe (2006), "Defining Asymmetric Warfare," *The Land Warfare Papers*, Association of the United States Army, Arlington, VA, https://www.ausa .org/publications/defining-asymmetric-warfare, and Sun Tzu, translated by Samuel B. Griffith (1971), *The Art of War* (London: Oxford University Press).

3. On terrorist cooperation, see Yonah Alexander and Dennis Pluchinsky (1992), *Europe's Red Terrorists: The Fighting Communist Organizations* (London: Frank Cass), and Bruce Hoffman (2006), *Inside Terrorism*, revised ed. (New York: Columbia University Press). On Air France Flight 139, see Edward F. Mickolus (1980), *Transnational Terrorism: A Chronology of Events, 1968–1979* (Westport, CT: Greenwood Press).

4. On al-Qaeda's leaderless jihad, consult Marc Sageman (2004), *Understanding Terror Networks* (Philadelphia, PA: University of Pennsylvania Press), and Marc Sageman (2008), *Leaderless Jihad: Terror Networks in the Twenty-First Century* (Philadelphia, PA: University of Pennsylvania Press).

5. Todd Sandler (2003), "Collective Action and Transnational Terrorism," *World Economy* 26 (6), 779–802, and Todd Sandler (2005), "Collective versus Unilateral Responses to Terrorism," *Public Choice* 124 (1–2), 75–93.

6. US Department of State (2001), *Patterns of Global Terrorism, 2001* (Washington, DC: US Department of State), p. 68.

7. Harvey E. Lapan and Todd Sandler (1993), "Terrorism and Signalling," *European Journal of Political Economy* 9 (3), 383–397, and Per Baltzer Overgaard (1994), "The Scale of Terrorist Attacks as a Signal of Resources," *Journal of Conflict Resolution* 38 (3), 452–478.

8. Facts are taken from Edward F. Mickolus, Todd Sandler, and Jean M. Murdock (1989), *International Terrorism in the 1980s: A Chronology of Events*, vol. 2, *1984–1987* (Ames, IA: Iowa State University Press), pp. 114–115. Their account is based on media reports.

9. On Damage Exchange Rates, see Martin Shubik and Aaron Zelinsky (2007), "Terrorism: Who Pays?," http://ssrn.com/ abstract=956403. On the cost of suicide vests, see Hoffman, *Inside Terrorism*.

10. Avinash Dixit, Susan Skeath, and David Reiley (2015), *Games of Strategy*, 4th ed. (New York: Norton), p. 62.

11. Vicki Bier, Santiago Oliveros, and Larry Samuelson (2007), "Choosing What to Protect: Strategic Defensive Allocation against an Unknown Attacker," *Journal of Public Economic Theory* 9 (4), 563–587.

12. Weakest-link and best-shot actions are discussed by Jack Hirshleifer (1983), "From the Weakest-Link to Best-Shot: The Voluntary Provision of Public Goods," *Public Choice* 41 (3), 371–386, and Todd Sandler (1997), *Global Challenges: An Approach to Environmental, Political, and Economic Problems* (Cambridge: Cambridge University Press).

13. Edward R. Mickolus (1993), *Terrorism, 1988–1991: A Chronology of Events and a Selectively Annotated Bibliography* (Westport, CT: Greenwood Press); see its update on the December 21, 1988, downing of Pan Am Flight 103.

14. Edward F. Mickolus (2008), *Terrorism, 2005–2007: A Chronology* (Westport, CT: Praeger Security International). On the forerunner of ISIS, see Daniel Byman (2015), *Al Qaeda, the Islamic State, and the Global Jihadist Movement: What Everyone Needs to Know* (New York: Oxford University Press). On bin Laden's letter see Kevin Siqueira and Todd Sandler (2010), "Terrorist Networks, Support, and Delegation," *Public Choice* 142 (1–2), 237–253.

15. Facts from this paragraph come from Mickolus, Sandler, and Murdock, *International Terrorism in the 1980s*, vol. 1, pp. 234–239.

16. Walter Enders and Paan Jindapon (2010), "Network Externalities and the Structure of Terror Networks," *Journal of Conflict Resolution* 54 (2), 262–280, and Walter Enders and Xuejuan Su (2007), "Rational Terrorists and Optimal Network Structure," *Journal of Conflict Resolution* 51 (1), 33–57.

17. The plane's late departure also helped because cell phone calls to passengers aboard Flight 93 alerted them to other skyjackings that day.

18. Hoffman, *Inside Terrorism*, pp. 119–127.

19. S. Brock Blomberg, Rozlyn C. Engel, and Reid Sawyer (2010), "On the Duration and Sustainability of Transnational Terrorist Organizations," *Journal of Conflict Resolution* 54 (2), 303–330, S. Brock Blomberg, Khusrav Gaibulloev, and Todd Sandler (2011), "Terrorist Group Survival: Ideology, Tactics, and Base of Operations," *Public Choice* 149 (3–4), 441–463, Khusrav Gaibulloev and Todd Sandler (2013), "Determinants of the Demise of Terrorist Organizations," *Southern Economic Journal*

79 (4), 774–792, and Brian J. Phillips (2014), "Terrorist Group Cooperation and Longevity," *International Studies Quarterly* 58 (2), 336–347.

20. Walter Enders and Todd Sandler (2012), *The Political Economy of Terrorism*, 2nd ed. (New York: Cambridge University Press).

21. US Government Accountability Office (2010), "Homeland Security: Better Use of Terrorist Watchlist Information and Improvements in Deployment of Passenger Screening Checkpoint Technologies Could Further Strengthen Security," GAO-10-401T, US Government Accountability Office, Washington, DC.

22. National Commission on Terrorist Attacks upon the United States (2004), *The 9/11 Commission Report* (New York: Norton).

23. Jack Hirshleifer (1991), "The Paradox of Power," *Economics & Politics* 3 (3), 177–200.

Chapter 6

1. Edward F. Mickolus, Todd Sandler, and Jean M. Murdock (1989), *International Terrorism in the 1980s: A Chronology of Events*, vol. 2, *1984–1987* (Ames, IA: Iowa State University Press), p. 595.

2. Walter Enders and Todd Sandler (2012), *The Political Economy of Terrorism*, 2nd ed. (New York: Cambridge University Press), and Brian A. Jackson, Lloyd Dixon, and Victoria A. Greenfield (2007), *Economically Targeted Terrorism: A Review of the Literature and a Framework for Considering Defensive Approaches*, Rand Center for Terrorism Risk Management Policy, Technical Report (Santa Monica CA: Rand).

3. Edward F. Mickolus (1980), *Transnational Terrorism: A Chronology of Events, 1968–1979* (Westport, CT: Greenwood Press), pp. 721–724.

4. Damage from the Bishopsgate bombing is sometimes estimated to be over one billion pounds sterling. On this bombing, see Edward F. Mickolus and Susan L. Simmons (1997), *Terrorism, 1992–1995: A Chronology of Events and a Selectively Annotated Bibliography* (Westport, CT: Greenwood Press). Also see Jackson, Dixon, and Greenfield, *Economically Targeted Terrorism*.

5. Jackson, Dixon, and Greenfield, *Economically Targeted Terrorism*.

6. These counts come from Edward F. Mickolus, Todd Sandler, Jean M. Murdock, and Peter Flemming (2016), *International Terrorism: Attributes of Terrorist Events, 1968–2015* (ITERATE) (Ponte Vedra, FL: Vinyard Software).

7. Enders and Sandler, *The Political Economy of Terrorism*, Todd Sandler (2014), "The Analytical Study of Terrorism: Taking Stock," *Journal of Peace Research* 51 (2), 257–271, and Todd Sandler and Walter Enders (2008), "Economic Consequences of Terrorism in Developed and Developing Countries: An Overview," in *Terrorism, Economic Development and Political Openness*, edited by Philip Keefer and Norma Loayza, pp. 17–47 (New York: Cambridge University Press).

8. Jackson, Dixon, and Greenfield, *Economically Targeted Terrorism*, and Sandler and Enders, "Economic Consequences of Terrorism in Developed and Developing Countries."

9. Edward F. Mickolus and Susan L. Simmons (2005), *Terrorism, 2002–2004: A Chronology* (Westport, CT: Praeger Security International).

10. On the greater adverse effect of transnational terrorism compared to domestic terrorism, see Subhayu Bandyopadhyay, Todd Sandler, and Javed Younas (2014), "Foreign Direct Investment, Aid, and Terrorism," *Oxford Economic Papers* 66 (1), 25–50, Khusrav Gaibulloev and Todd Sandler (2008), "Growth Consequences of Terrorism in Western Europe," *Kyklos* 61 (3), 411–424, and Khusrav Gaibulloev and Todd Sandler (2011), "The Adverse Effect of Transnational and Domestic Terrorism on Growth in Africa," *Journal of Peace Research* 48 (3), 355–371.

11. Howard Kunreuther and Erwann Michel-Kerjan (2004), "Policy Watch: Challenge for Terrorism Risk Insurance in the United States," *Journal of Economic Perspectives* 18 (4), 201–214, and Howard Kunreuther, Erwann Michel-Kerjan, and Beverly Porter (2003), "Assessing, Managing and Financing Extreme Events: Dealing with Terrorism," Working Paper 10179, National Bureau of Economic Research, Cambridge, MA.

12. Bureau of Economic Analysis (2001), "Business Situation," *Survey of Current Business* 81 (11), 2–3, https://fraser.stlouisfed.org/files/docs/publications/SCB/2000-09/SCB_112001.pdf.

13. Mikel Busea, Aurelia Valiño, Joost Heijs, Thomas Baumert, and Javier Gonzalez Gomez (2007), "The Economic Cost of March 11: Measuring Direct Economic Cost of the Terrorist Attack on March 11, 2004 in Madrid," *Terrorism and Political Violence* 19 (4), 489–509.

14. The material for this and the next paragraph is supported by Enders and Sandler, *The Political Economy of Terrorism*,

pp. 294–298, and Sandler and Enders, "Economic Consequences of Terrorism in Developed and Developing Countries," pp. 26–28.

15. The material in this section relies on the excellent study, Andrew H. Chen and Thomas F. Siems (2004), "The Effects of Terrorism on Global Capital Markets," *European Journal of Political Economy* 20 (2), 349–366. See also Rafi Eldor and Rafi Melnick (2004), "Financial Markets and Terrorism," *European Journal of Political Economy* 20 (2), 367–386, and Konstantinos Drakos (2004), "Terrorism-Induced Structural Shifts in Financial Risk: Airline Stocks in the Aftermath of the September 11th Terror Attacks," *European Journal of Political Economy* 20 (2), 435–466.

16. Chen and Siems, "The Effects of Terrorism on Global Capital Markets."

17. Peter Gordon, James E. Moore II, Harry W. Richardson, and Qisheng Pan (2005), "The Economic Impact of a Terrorist Attack on the Twin Ports of Los Angeles–Long Beach," in *The Economic Impacts of Terrorist Attacks*, edited by Harry W. Richardson, Peter Gordon, and James E. Moore II, pp. 262–286 (Cheltenham, UK: Edward Elgar).

18. Drakos, "Terrorism-Induced Structural Shifts in Financial Risk."

19. Eldor and Melnick, "Financial Markets and Terrorism."

20. S. Brock Blomberg, Gregory D. Hess, and Athanasios Orphanides (2004), "The Macroeconomic Consequences of Terrorism," *Journal of Monetary Economics* 51 (5), 1007–1032.

21. Gaibulloev and Sandler, "Growth Consequences of Terrorism in Western Europe," Khusrav Gaibulloev and Todd Sandler (2009), "The Impact of Terrorism and Conflicts on Growth in Asia," *Economics & Politics* 21 (3), 359–383, Gaibulloev and Sandler, "The Adverse Effect of Transnational and Domestic Terrorism on Growth in Africa," and Jose Tavares (2004), "Open Society Assesses Its Enemies: Shocks, Disasters and Terrorist Attacks," *Journal of Monetary Economics* 51 (5), 1039–1070.

22. Khusrav Gaibulloev, Todd Sandler, and Donggyu Sul (2014), "Dynamic Panel Analysis under Cross-Sectional Dependence," *Political Analysis* 22 (2), 258–273.

23. Alberto Abadie and Javier Gardeazabal (2003), "The Economic Cost of Conflict: A Case Study of the Basque Country," *American Economic Review* 93 (1), 113–132, and Zvi Eckstein and Daniel Tsiddon (2004), "Macroeconomic Consequences of Terror: Theory

and the Case of Israel," *Journal of Monetary Economics* 51 (5), 971–1002.

24. Javed Younas and Todd Sandler (2017), "Gender Imbalance and Terrorism in Developing Countries," *Journal of Conflict Resolution* 61 (3), 483–510.

25. Mickolus and Simmons, *Terrorism, 2002–2004.*

26. United States Department of State Fact Sheet (2002), "Yemen: The Economic Cost of Terrorism," https://2001-2009.state.gov/s/ct/rls/fs/2002/15028.htm.

27. Walter Enders and Todd Sandler (1991), "Causality between Transnational Terrorism and Tourism: The Case of Spain," *Terrorism* 14 (1), 49–58.

28. Walter Enders, Todd Sandler, and Gerald F. Parise (1992), "An Econometric Analysis of the Impact of Terrorism on Tourism," *Kyklos* 45 (4), 531–554.

29. Konstantinos Drakos and Ali M. Kutan (2003), "Regional Effects of Terrorism on Tourism in Three Mediterranean Countries," *Journal of Conflict Resolution* 47 (5), 621–641.

30. See, for example, Harumi Ito and Darin Lee (2005), "Assessing the Impact of the September 11 Terrorist Attacks on US Airline Demand," *Journal of Economics and Business* 57 (1), 79–95, Abraham Pizam and Aliza Fleischer (2002), "Severity versus Frequency of Acts of Terrorism: Which Has a Larger Impact on Tourism Demand?," *Journal of Travel Research* 40 (3), 337–339, and Brian W. Sloboda (2003), "Assessing the Effects of Terrorism on Tourism by the Use of Time Series Methods," *Tourism Economics* 9 (2), 179–190.

31. Eric Neumayer and Thomas Plümper (2016), "Spatial Spillovers from Terrorism on Tourism: Western Victims in Islamic Destination Countries," *Public Choice* 169 (1–2), 195–206.

32. Walter Enders and Todd Sandler (1996), "Terrorism and Foreign Direct Investment in Spain and Greece," *Kyklos* 49 (3), 331–352.

33. See Alberto Abadie and Javier Gardeazabal (2008), "Terrorism and the World Economy," *European Economic Review* 52 (1), 1–27, Bandyopadhyay, Sandler, and Younas, "Foreign Direct Investment, Aid, and Terrorism," and Walter Enders, Adolfo Sachsida, and Todd Sandler (2006), "The Impact of Transnational Terrorism on US Foreign Direct Investment," *Political Research Quarterly* 59 (4), 517–531.

34. Subhayu Bandyopadhyay, Todd Sandler, and Javed Younas (2017), "Trade and Terrorism: A Disaggregate Approach," unpublished manuscript, Center for Global Collective Action, University of Texas at Dallas, Richardson, TX, S. Brock Blomberg and Gregory D. Hess (2006), "How Much Does Violence Tax Trade?," *Review of Economics and Statistics* 88 (4), 599–612, José De Sousa, Daniel Mirza, and Thierry Verdier (2009), "Trade and the Spillovers of Transnational Terrorism," *Swiss Journal of Economics and Statistics* 145 (4), 453–461, Daniel Mirza and Thierry Verdier (2014), "Are Lives a Substitute for Livelihoods? Terrorism, Security, and US Bilateral Imports," *Journal of Conflict Resolution* 58 (6), 943–975, and Volker Nitsch and Dieter Schumacher (2004), "Terrorism and International Trade: An Empirical Investigation," *European Journal of Political Economy* 20 (2), 423–433.

35. Sandler and Enders, "Economic Consequences of Terrorism in Developed and Developing Countries."

36. Axel Dreher, Daniel Meierrieks, and Tim Krieger (2011), "Hit and (They Will) Run: The Impact of Terrorism on Migration," *Economics Letters* 113 (1), 42–46.

Chapter 7

1. See, for example, Bruce Hoffman (1997), "The Confluence of International and Domestic Trends in Terrorism," *Terrorism and Political Violence* 9 (1), 1–15, and Bruce Hoffman (1998), "Terrorism Trends and Prospects," in *Countering the New Terrorism*, edited by Ian O. Lesser, Bruce Hoffman, John Arquilla, David Ronfeldt, and Michele Zanini, pp. 7–38 (Santa Monica, CA: Rand).

2. Examples of this technique can be found in Walter Enders and Todd Sandler (1999), "Transnational Terrorism in the Post–Cold War Era," *International Studies Quarterly* 43 (2), 145–167, Walter Enders and Todd Sandler (2000), "Is Transnational Terrorism Becoming More Threatening? A Time-Series Investigation," *Journal of Conflict Resolution* 44 (3), 307–332, and Walter Enders and Todd Sandler (2005), "Transnational Terrorism 1968–2000: Thresholds, Persistence, and Forecasts," *Southern Economic Journal* 71 (3), 467–482.

3. Enders and Sandler, "Is Transnational Terrorism Becoming More Threatening?"

4. The journal's editor was Bruce Russett from Yale University. He felt, like us, that the title accurately reflected the article's analysis.

5. Beom S. Lee, Walter Enders, and Todd Sandler (2009), "9/11: What Did We Know and When Did We Know It?" *Defence and Peace Economics* 20 (2), 79–93.

6. These translated quotations of Osama bin Laden come from National Commission on Terrorist Attacks Upon the United States (2004), *The 9/11 Commission Report* (New York: Norton).

7. Lee, Enders, and Sandler, "9/11."

8. Edward F. Mickolus (2008), *Terrorism, 2005–2007: A Chronology* (Westport, CT: Praeger Security International).

9. P. W. Singer and Allan Friedman (2014), *Cybersecurity and Cyberwar: What Everyone Needs to Know* (Oxford: Oxford University Press), p. 96.

10. Singer and Friedman, *Cybersecurity and Cyberwar*, p. 96.

11. Singer and Friedman, *Cybersecurity and Cyberwar*, p. 106.

12. Facts come from Walter Enders and Todd Sandler (2012), *The Political Economy of Terrorism*, 2nd ed. (New York: Cambridge University Press), pp. 350–352.

13. John Arquilla and David Ronfeldt (eds.) (2001), *Networks and Netwars* (Santa Monica, CA: Rand), Walter Enders and Paan Jindapon (2010), "Network Externalities and the Structure of Terror Networks," *Journal of Conflict Resolution* 54 (2), 262–280, Walter Enders and Xuejuan Su (2007), "Rational Terrorists and Optimal Network Structure," *Journal of Conflict Resolution* 51 (1), 33–57, and Jonathan D. Farley (2003), "Breaking al Qaeda: A Mathematical Analysis of Counterterrorism Operations," *Studies in Conflict & Terrorism* 26 (6), 399–411.

14. Robert Bunker (2000), "Weapons of Mass Disruption and Terrorism," *Terrorism and Political Violence* 12 (1), 37–46.

15. Bruce Hoffman (2006), *Inside Terrorism*, revised ed. (New York: Columbia University Press), pp. 124–126, and Edward F. Mickolus and Susan L. Simmons (1997), *Terrorism, 1992–1995: A Chronology of Events and a Selectively Annotated Bibliography* (Westport, CT: Greenwood Press).

16. Peter Gordon, James E. Moore II, Harry W. Richardson, and Qisheng Pan (2005), "The Economic Impact of a Terrorist Attack on the Twin Ports of Los Angeles–Long Beach," in *The Economic Impacts of Terrorist Attacks*, edited by Harry W. Richardson, Peter Gordon, and James E. Moore II, pp. 262–286 (Cheltenham, UK: Edward Elgar).

17. Gary Ackerman (2004), "WMD Terrorism Research: Where to from Here?," unpublished manuscript, Center for Nonproliferation Studies, Monterey Institute of International Studies, Monterey, CA, Kate Ivanova and Todd Sandler (2006), "CBRN Incidents: Political Regimes, Perpetrators, and Targets," *Terrorism and Political Violence* 18 (3), 423–448, and Kate Ivanova and Todd Sandler (2007), "CBRN Attack Perpetrators: An Empirical Study," *Foreign Policy Analysis* 3 (4), 273–294.

18. Institute of Medicine (2002), *Biological Threats and Terrorism: Assessing the Science and Response Capabilities* (Washington, DC: National Academy Press).

19. Hoffman, *Inside Terrorism*, pp. 124–125, and Edward F. Mickolus and Susan L. Simmons (2002), *Terrorism, 1996–2001: A Chronology* (Westport, CT: Greenwood Press).

20. Hoffman, *Inside Terrorism*, p. 125.

21. Hoffman, *Inside Terrorism*, p. 123.

22. Hoffman, *Inside Terrorism*, pp. 123–124.

23. Ivanova and Sandler, "CBRN Incidents," and Ivanova and Sandler, "CBRN Attack Perpetrators."

24. This incident is described in greater detail in https://www.cnn.com/2016/03/18/us/university-of-california-merced-stabbings-terror-inspired-fbi/index.html.

25. Edward F. Mickolus, *Terrorism Worldwide, 2016* (Jefferson, NC: McFarland).

26. *The Guardian* (2000), "What Really Happened on Flight 103?," https://www.theguardian.com/uk/2000/feb/27/lockerbie.life1.

27. *The Guardian*, "What Really Happened on Flight 103?"

INDEX